NON-CHRISTI.

SYST

CONFUCIANISM

AND

TAOUISM.

WITH A MAP.

BY

ROBERT K. DOUGLAS,

OF THE BRITISH MUSEUM, AND PROFESSOR OF CHINESE AT
KING'S COLLEGE, LONDON.

FIFTH EDITION.

PUBLISHED UNDER THE DIRECTION OF THE GENERAL
LITERATURE COMMITTEE.

LONDON:

SOCIETY FOR PROMOTING CHRISTIAN KNOWLEDGE,

NORTHUMBERLAND AVENUE, W.C.; 43, QUEEN VICTORIA STREET, E.C.

NEW YORK: E. & J. B. YOUNG & CO.

1900.

London: Published by the Society for Promoting Christian Knowledge.

Keaung River

Han Kong River

Wei River

Han River

Ho (River)

Ho River

TSIN

TS IN

T S O O

YUEH

WOO OO

CHING

ROYAL DOMAIN OR CHING

SUNG

TSEU

CHOO

KE

TSE

Ho (River)

YEN

PEKING

Keang R.

PREFACE.

THE present volume contains a new survey of wide subjects for inquiry. The number of native authors whose writings it would be necessary to master in the preparation of a work *de novo* on Confucianism and Taouism is so great that it renders the accomplishment of such a task by any one author next to impossible. It has been necessary therefore for me to take advantage of the labours of preceding European workers in the separate fields, as well as of Chinese writers not previously consulted. In the first category I have to acknowledge the very material assistance I have derived from Legge's "Chinese Classics," Faber's "Systematic Digest of the Doctrines of Confucius," translated from the German by P. G. Von Moellendorf; Johnson's "Oriental Religious China"; Watters' "Lao-tzu"; "The Speculations of 'the old Philosopher,' Lau-tsze," by Chalmers; Julien's "Le Livre de la Voie et de la Vertu"; and "Le Livre des Récompenses et des Peines," by the same Author.

References to the native works above alluded to will be found in the foot-notes.

ROBERT K. DOUGLAS.

CONTENTS.

———◆◆———

CONFUCIANISM.

TAOUISM.

TAOUISM.

CONFUCIANISM.

CONFUCIANISM.

CHAPTER I.

INTRODUCTORY.

CONFUCIUS was not an original thinker. To quote his own words, "he was a transmitter, and not a maker;" and in order therefore rightly to understand his teachings, and the effect they have produced, it is necessary to glance at the early history of the Chinese people, and to gain some acquaintance with the sources from which Confucius drew his inspiration.

The earliest records of the Chinese which have been handed down to us represent them as a small tribe of wanderers camping in the primeval forests which then covered the district which is now known as the Province of Shanse. That they were not natives of the soil, but were pilgrims and strangers in the land, has been abundantly proved; and one of the most striking evidences of this is found in the fact, that no strivings after the beginnings of knowledge are to be traced either in the literature or the traditions of China. At our first introduction to the people, we find them already possessed of a considerable acquaintance with the arts and sciences. It is natural, therefore, that we should look abroad for a contemporary nation occupying the same plane of knowledge,

with whom they may have been brought into contact,
and such an one we meet with in the country north of
the Persian Gulf. From the Babylonian tablets we
learn that the dwellers in Elam and Chaldea enjoyed
in many and striking particulars precisely the same
knowledge as that which we find existing at the first
on the banks of the Yellow River. It is incontestable,
also, that many of the earliest Chinese characters are
derived from the cuneiform writing of Babylonia, and
Mr. C. J. Ball has done much to prove that Chinese
is very nearly related to the ancient language of
Akkadia. But one of the most interesting evidences
on the point is furnished by the explanation of a
strange astronomical anomaly, which appears at first
sight quite unintelligible. In one of the earliest
chapters of the *Shoo King*, or Book of History,
astronomical indications are given, which imply the
shifting of the cardinal points towards the west.
That is to say, that the orientation described, represents the north as being in reality the north-
west, and the south the south-east, and so on.
The only explanations of this displacement which,
until lately, have been offered, have cast reflections
on the astronomical knowledge of "the intelligent
and accomplished" Emperor Yaou (2356 B.C.). But,
as Dr. de Lacouperie has pointed out, the cuneiform tablets have revealed the fact, that precisely
the same shifting of the points of the compass
existed among the Akkadians. It is remarkable also
to find, in confirmation of this discovery, that,
according to the same scholar, all the Chaldean
monuments, with the exception of the temple of

Bel-Merodach at Babylon, are orientated with the same inclination towards the west.

It was then from the habitat thus indicated that the Chinese migrated, and moving probably along the southern slope of the T'eenshan range, finally reached the northern bend of the Yellow River in latitude 41°. Here, after a weary journey through the Mongolian Desert, they entered upon a rich and productive land where scarcely any labour was demanded by the soil from the emigrant, and where the rain, attracted by the tree-clad mountains, fell in regular and temperate showers upon the growing grain.

This "garden of China," as it has been called, was then the first home of the Chinese in the "Middle Kingdom." But they were far from being allowed to take possession of the land unopposed. Like the Israelites of old, they found a land flowing with milk and honey, but also, like them, they had to fight their way, step by step, against the tribal possessors of the soil. The barbarous weapons and disjointed action, however, of the "Hordes of the North," "of the South," "of the East," and "of the West," who were their foes, were unable to resist the superior civilization and cohesion of the Chinese, and gradually as these advanced on to the plains the retreating "barbarians" sought shelter among the mountains. But in the presence of even such enemies it was necessary that the settlement of the country should be undertaken with caution, and as the main body pushed on, colonies were planted at strategical points on its course under the direction of chiefs, or "Pastors of Men," as Mencius calls them.

The native records of events at this early period are not to be treated as history, and it is not until we reach the reign of Yaou (2356 B.C.) that we exchange the purest fable for even doubtful history. It is at this point that the *Shoo King,* or "Book of History," edited by Confucius, commences. "Anciently there was an Emperor Yaou," writes the editor, " all-informed, intelligent, accomplished, and thoughtful ;" and if we are to accept the received account of his reign, this description does not do more than justice to his character. His first care, we are told, was to advance the able and virtuous to offices in the state, and finally he united and harmonized the myriad states of the empire ; and, lo ! the black-haired people were transformed. He appointed astronomers to calculate and delineate the movements and appearances of the sun, the moon, the stars, and the zodiacal spaces ; and he then determined the four seasons and the length of the year. He adopted intercalary months, and the calendar he arranged is that which is still in use in China.

On the death of Yaou, Shun, who had shared his throne for some years, succeeded as sole emperor. Like his predecessor, he was " profound, wise, accomplished, and intelligent. He was mild, respectful, and quite sincere. The report of his mysterious virtue was heard on high, and he was appointed to take the throne." One of his first public acts, after having still further perfected the astronomical calculations of Yaou, was to sacrifice to Shang-te, the Supreme Ruler or God. "Thereafter," we are told, " he sacrificed specially, but with the ordinary forms, to Shang-te ; sacrificed with purity and reverence to the six Honoured Ones ; offered appropriate sacrifices to the hills and rivers; and extended his worship to the host of spirits."[1] This is the first mention we have in Chinese history of religious worship, though the expressions used plainly imply that the worship of Shang-te at least had previously existed. It is to this Supreme Being that all the highest forms of adoration have been offered in all ages. By His decree kings were made and rulers executed judgment. In His hands were the issues of life and death, and he whom He blessed was blessed, and he whom He cursed was cursed. In all probability there was a time when the worship of Shang-te was the expression of the pure monotheistic faith of the Chinese. By degrees, however, corruptions crept in, and though Shang-te always remained the supreme object of veneration, they saw no disloyalty to him in rendering homage to the powers of nature which they learnt to personify, and to the spirits of their departed ancestors, who were supposed to guard and watch over, in a subordinate manner, the welfare of their descendants.

During this reign the empire was divided into twelve provinces, and ministers of agriculture, crime, works, forests, religious worship, and of music were appointed. That the standard of morality was high, even at this early period, appears from the conversations which are reported between Shun's vice-regent Yu and one of his advisers. In answer to the question put by

---

[1] Shoo king. Shun-teen.

Yu, "What are the nine virtues?" the minister replied, "Affability combined with dignity; mildness combined with firmness; bluntness combined with respectfulness; aptness for government, combined with reverence; docility combined with boldness; straightforwardness combined with gentleness; easiness combined with discrimination; vigour combined with sincerity; and valour combined with righteousness."[1]

But though the excellence attributed to the early sovereigns of China appears much overwrought, an argument for its justice may be found in the fact that an equally overwhelming condemnation is reserved for the later sovereigns of the dynasty, which had its origin in the reigns of Yaou and Shun. Gradually the high standard of morality which had distinguished those emperors disappeared under the rule of their successors, until licentiousness, disorder, and anarchy reached their height under the infamous tyrant Këĕ Wang, who ascended the throne in the year 1818 B.C. This "injurer of men and destroyer of many," as he was called, exhausted both the men and means of his empire by constant wars with the neighbouring states. Under his rule the affairs of government were neglected, and the people cried aloud for relief from the tyranny to which they were subjected. A comparison between the disorder which reigned in their own provinces and the quiet contentment of the people of the neighbouring state of Shang could not but force itself on the unfortunate subjects of Këĕ,

---

[1] Shoo king. Kaou-yaou mow.

who sighed for the gentle rule of King T'ang. At last the tyranny of the despot became unbearable, and in 1765 B.C. T'ang appealed to the people to rise against their oppressor, but at the same time he took care to explain to them that it was as the instrument of Heaven, and not as a rebel, that he took up arms. "It is not I," said he, "the little child, who dare to undertake what may seem to be a rebellious enterprise ; but for the many crimes of the sovereign of Hea, Heaven has commanded me to destroy him." [1]

The struggle was of short duration. On one side were justice and strong battalions, and on the other divided counsels and disheartened defenders. But to the last Kĕĕ professed to feel perfectly secure. "Has ever the sun perished?" said he to his people. "If the sun perish, then I and you will also perish." Legend says that in the final battle this phenomenon actually occurred. Two suns fought in the sky, and one was devoured by the other. The earth shook and rivers were dried up. Kĕĕ's troops were utterly routed, and the fallen emperor remained a prisoner in the hands of T'ang. In the person of the conqueror appeared a reflection of the virtues of Yaou and Shun. Harmony and tranquillity pervaded the empire, agriculture flourished, and the blessings of Heaven rested on the land. By degrees, however, his successors fell short of his example, until P'an-kăng ascended the throne in 1401 B.C. For a time this sovereign restored prosperity to the country. He put an end to the abuses which had arisen, and created

---

[1] Shoo king, T'ang She.

a new starting-point for his dynasty by changing its title from Shang to Yin, the name of the new capital which he established on the south of the Yellow River.

With the death of P'an-kăng the country again fell into disorder, which reached its height under the " dissolute, intemperate, reckless, oppressive " Show (1154 B.C.—1122). As at the close of the last dynasty so now, a leader arose who drew all men unto him, and claiming the same Heaven-sent mission as that fulfilled by T'ang, the king of Chow took the field against the tyrant. Addressing the people, he said, " Show, the king of Shang, does not reverence Heaven above, and inflicts calamities on the people below. He has abandoned himself to drunkenness, and is reckless in lust. . . . . He has made it his pursuit to have palaces, towers, pavilions, embankments, ponds, and all other extravagancies, to the most painful injury of you, the myriad people. He has burnt and roasted the loyal and good. . . . . He abides squatting on his heels, not serving Shang-te or the Spirits of Heaven and Earth, neglecting also the temple of his ancestors, and not sacrificing in it. . . . . The iniquity of Shang is full. Heaven gives command to destroy it. . . . . I, who am a little child, early and late am filled with apprehensions. I have received charge from my deceased father Wăn ; I have offered special sacrifice to God ; I have performed the due service to the great Earth, and I lead the multitude of you to execute the punishment appointed by Heaven."

This summons was eagerly responded to, not only

by the immediate followers of Woo-Wang, but by the men of the neighbouring tribes. One battle decided the issue of the contest. Show's troops were utterly routed, and the tyrant finding all lost, burned himself to death, leaving his followers and empire at the mercy of the victor. With the energy of a reformer Woo remodelled the State on its ancient lines. He dispossessed all incompetent holders of office, and promoted only those who proved themselves worthy and able. " He attached great importance to the people being taught the duties of the five relations of society, to their being well fed, and to the proper observance of funeral ceremonies and of sacrifices. He showed the reality of his truthfulness, and proved clearly his righteousness. He honoured virtue, and rewarded merit. Then he had only to let his robes fall down, and fold his hands, and the empire was governed."

The conquest of the turbulent state of Shang having been thus accomplished, communication with the western border tribes was re-established, and amongst others the people of Leu came to pay their homage and to acknowledge their fealty by a present of hounds. These the king would have accepted, but the imperial guardian dissuaded him from doing so on grounds which are identical with those on which the Chinese government of the present day has steadily refused to accept the inventions and advice proffered to it by foreigners. " The intelligent kings," he said, " have paid careful attention to their virtue, and the wild tribes on every side have willingly acknowledged subjection to them. . . . . Complete virtue allows no contemptuous familiarity. . . . . A

prince should not value strange things to the con-
temning things that are useful, and then his people
will be able to supply all his needs. . . . . Even dogs
and horses, which are not native to his country, he
will not keep ; fine birds and strange animals he will
not nourish in his kingdom. *When he does not look
on foreign things as precious, foreigners will come to
him ;* when it is work which is precious to him, then his
own people will enjoy repose." These maxims, which
are held to embalm the highest wisdom, have been
carefully acted upon by all virtuous sovereigns, and from
a Chinese point of view the effect has been excellent.
This proud spirit of self-containment has done much
to maintain the spirit of adulation with which China
has been regarded by the surrounding nations for so
many centuries.

But King Woo had an even more powerful adviser
than the Imperial Guardian in the person of his
younger brother, the Duke of Chow. His conduct
in the first incident in which his name occurs marks
him as a man of strong character, and supplies the
first instance on record of the worship of ancestors.
Two years after the conquest of Shang it chanced
that King Woo fell ill, and was like to die. Whereupon the courtiers proposed to divine by the tortoise
what should be the end of his illness, but Chow for-
bad this, and having built three altars of earth facing
the south, one for his father, one for his grandfather,
and one for his great-grandfather, he stood opposite
the fourth, which faced the north, and prayed thus :—
" Your chief descendant is suffering from a severe
and dangerous illness ; if you three kings have in

heaven the charge of watching over him, let me suffer for him. I have been lovingly obedient to my father; I am possessed of many abilities and arts which fit me to serve spiritual beings. Your chief descendant, on the other hand, has not so many abilities and arts as I, and is not so capable of serving spiritual beings. And moreover he was appointed in the hall of God to extend his aid to the four quarters of the empire, so that he might establish your descendants in this lower world. . . . . Oh, do not let that precious Heaven-conferred appointment fall to the ground, and all our former kings will have a perpetual reliance and resort. I will now seek your orders from the great tortoise. If you grant my request, I will take these symbols and this mace (emblems of the Imperial House of Chow) and return and wait for the issue ; but if you do not grant it, I will put them by," *i.e.*, the death of King Woo would be the signal for the fall of the dynasty, and there would therefore be no further use for the regalia. On this occasion the king recovered, but death soon afterwards overtook him, and under his successor the empire was divided into two portions, over one of which the Duke of Chow was appointed to preside.

On taking over the reins of government, the duke issued a proclamation to the people of Yin, in which he briefly summed up the history of the two preceding dynasties in these words :—" I have heard the saying, ' Shang-te leads man to tranquil security;' but the sovereign of Hea would not move to such security, thereupon Te (God) sent down correction, indicating his mind to him. Këĕ, however, would not be warned by Te, but proceeded to greater dissoluteness, and sloth, and excuses for himself. Then Heaven no longer regarded nor heard him, but disallowed his great appointment, and inflicted extreme punishment. Hereupon It charged your founder, T'ang the Successful, to set Hea aside, and by means of able men to rule the empire. From T'ang the Successful down to the Emperor Yïh, every sovereign sought to make his virtue illustrious, and duly attended to the sacrifices. And thus it was that, while Heaven executed a great establishing influence, preserving and regulating the house of Yin, its sovereigns, on their part, were humbly careful not to lose the favour of God, and strove to manifest a good-doing corresponding to that of Heaven. But in these times, their successor showed himself greatly ignorant of the ways of Heaven. . . . Greatly abandoned to dissolute idleness, he paid no regard to the bright principles of Heaven, nor the awfulness of the people. On this account Shang-te no longer protected him, but sent down the great ruin which we have witnessed. Heaven was not with him because he did not seek to illustrate his virtue. . . . The sovereigns of our Chow, by their great goodness, were charged with the work of Te. They were charged to cut off Yin. They have now done it, and announced the correcting work to God. In our affairs we have followed no double aims :—ye of the royal house of Yin must follow us." Thus was again brought out prominently the doctrine, reiterated by Confucius, that a king's title to his throne lasted only as long as he followed the dictates of

Heaven, and that when he swerved persistently from the right course it was competent for the people to dethrone him.   On the virtue and wisdom of the Duke of Chow Confucius was never tired of expatiating, and he looked upon it as a sign of his failing powers when he ceased to dream of his great model.

To the duke succeeded Keun-ch'in in the vice-regal palace in the eastern capital, and the example of his illustrious predecessor was held up for his imitation in a long discourse addressed to him by the king on his taking office.   The influence of his example on the manners of the people was earnestly insisted on.   " You are the wind," said the king, " the inferior people are the grass."   The people, he was reminded, are born good, and it is the fault, therefore, of a ruler if he allows them by contact with evil to fall from the right way.   From all accounts Keun-ch'in was not an unworthy occupant of the great Duke's throne, and the empire was fairly prosperous down to the end of the reign of King Ching in 1079 B.C.

King K'ang, the son of this last monarch, next ascended the throne, but though he professed himself desirous of following in the footsteps of Wăn and Woo, who, as he said, were "greatly just and enriched the people," he failed to reach the standard of virtue which had been set up by those sovereigns. His reign was a long one, but before it came to a close in 1051 the seeds of division and strife which were so soon to bear fruit had already been sown. The Book of History is silent as to his death and the reign of his successor, Chaou; but the Historical Record, after mentioning the fact of the death of K'ang, says :—" During the reign of Chaou 'the Royal Path' was somewhat deflected. The king went on a tour of inspection on the southern frontier from which he never returned. He died on the river."

Of the next sovereign, Muh Wang, the Historical Record says that the Royal Path suffered a still further decline, and that the king encouraged a departure from the ways of Wăn and Woo. The most noteworthy action of his reign was the promulgation, when he was a hundred years old, of a penal code, under which he drew up a regular scale of fines for the redemption of punishments. For this the Chinese historians condemn him, as they consider that these enactments first opened the door to the system of official bribery and corruption which has produced such evils in China ever since.

Up to this point we have followed only the fortunes of the ruling state of Chow, since, until the accession of King Muh, when, as the Historical Record says, the ways of Kings Wăn and Woo were departed from, the history of that state may, speaking generally, be said to have been the history of the whole empire. But as the hold of the supreme sovereign over his vassals began to loosen, the princes of the various states into which the China of that day was divided became restless under control, and each sought to aggrandize himself at the expense of his neighbours, and of his loyalty to his sovereign.

At the time of which we write the Chinese were

still clinging to the banks of the Yellow River, along which they had first entered the country, and formed, within the limits of China proper, a few states on either shore lying between the 33rd and 38th parallels of latitude, and the 106th and 119th of longitude. The royal state of Chow occupied part of the modern province of Honan. To the north of this was the powerful state of Tsin, embracing the modern province of Shanse and part of Chili ; to the south was the barbarous state of T'soo, which stretched as far as the Yang-tsze-keang ; to the east, reaching to the coast, were a number of smaller states, among which those of Ts'e, Loo, Wei, Sung, and Ching were the chief ; and to the west of the Yellow River was the state of Ts'in, which was destined eventually to gain the mastery over the contending principalities.

On the establishment of the Chow dynasty, King Woo had apportioned these fiefships among members of his family, his adherents, and the descendants of some of the ancient virtuous kings. Each prince was empowered to administer his government as he pleased so long as he followed the general lines indicated by history ; and in the event of any act of aggression on the part of one state against another, the matter was to be reported to the king of the sovereign state, who was bound to punish the offender. It is plain that in such a system the elements of disorder must lie near the surface ; and no sooner was the authority of the central state lessened by the want of ability shown by the successors of Kings Woo, Ching, and K'ang, than constant strife broke out between the several chiefs. The hand of every man was against his neighbour, and the smaller states suffered the usual fate, under like circumstances, of being encroached upon and absorbed, notwithstanding their appeals for help to their common sovereign. The House of Chow having been thus found wanting, the device was resorted to of appointing one of the most powerful princes as a presiding chief, who should exercise royal functions, leaving the king only the title and paraphernalia of sovereignty. In fact, the China of this period was governed and administered very much as Japan was up till about twenty years ago. For Mikado, Shogun, and ruling Daimios, read King, presiding Chief, and Princes, and the parallel is as nearly as possible complete. The result of the system, however, in the two countries was different, for apart from the support received by the Mikado from the belief in his heavenly origin, the insular position of Japan prevented the possibility of the advent of elements of disorder from without, whereas the principalities of China were surrounded by semi-barbarous states, the chiefs of which were engaged in constant warfare with them.

Confucius's deep spirit of loyalty to the House of Chow forbade his following in the Book of History the careers of the sovereigns who reigned between the death of Muh in 946 B.C. and the accession of P'ing in 770. One after another these kings rose, reigned, and died, leaving each to his successor an ever-increasing heritage of woe. During the reign of Seuen (827–781) a gleam of light seems to have shot through the pervading darkness. Though falling far short of the excellencies of the founders of the dynasty, he yet strove to follow, though at a long interval, the examples they had set him ; and according to the Chinese belief, as an acknowledgment from Heaven of his efforts in the direction of virtue, it was given him to sit upon the throne for nearly half a century.

His successor, Yew, " the Dark," appears to even less advantage. No redeeming acts relieve the general disorder of his reign, and at the instigation of a favourite concubine he is said to have committed acts which place him on a level with Kёё and Show. Earthquakes, storms, and astrological portents appeared as in the dark days at the close of the Hea and Shang dynasties. His capital was surrounded by the barbarian allies of the Prince of Shin, the father of his wife, whom he had dismissed at the request of his favourite, and in an attempt to escape he fell a victim to their weapons.

With this event the Western Chow dynasty was brought to a close.

Here, also, the Book of History comes to an end, and the Spring and Autumn Annals by Confucius takes up the tale of iniquity and disorder which overspread the land. No more dreadful record of a nation's struggles can be imagined than that contained in Confucius's history. The country was torn by discord and desolated by wars. Husbandry was neglected, the peace of households was destroyed, and plunder and rapine were the watchwords of the time.

CHAPTER II

LIFE OF CONFUCIUS.

SUCH was the state of China at the time of the birth of Confucius (B.C. 551). Of the parents of the Sage we know but little, except that his father, Shuh-leang Heïh, was a military officer, eminent for his commanding stature, his great bravery, and immense strength, and that his mother's name was Yen Ching-tsai. The marriage of this couple took place when Heïh was seventy years old, and the prospect, therefore, of his having an heir having been but slight, unusual rejoicings commemorated the birth of the son, who was destined to achieve such everlasting fame.

Report says that the child was born in a cave on Mount Ne, whither Ching-tsai went in obedience to a vision to be confined. But this is but one of the many legends with which Chinese historians love to surround the birth of Confucius. With the same desire to glorify the Sage, and in perfect good faith, they narrate how the event was heralded by strange portents and miraculous appearances, how genii announced to Ching-tsai the honour that was in store for her, and how fairies attended at his nativity.

Of the early years of Confucius we have but scanty

record. It would seem that from his childhood he showed ritualistic tendencies, and we are told that as a boy he delighted to play at the arrangement of vessels and at postures of ceremony. As he advanced in years he became an earnest student of history, and looked back with love and reverence to the time when the great and good Yaou and Shun reigned in

" A golden age, fruitful of golden deeds."

At the age of fifteen "he bent his mind to learning," and when he was nineteen years old he married a lady from the state of Sung. As has befallen many other great men, Confucius's married life was not a happy one, and he finally divorced his wife, not, however, before she had borne him a son.

Soon after his marriage, at the instigation of poverty, Confucius accepted the office of keeper of the stores of grain, and in the following year he was promoted to be guardian of the public fields and lands. It was while holding this latter office that his son was born, and so well known and highly esteemed had he already become that the reigning duke, on hearing of the event, sent him a present of a carp, from which circumstance the infant derived his name, Le ("a carp"). The name of this son seldom occurs in the life of his illustrious father, and the few references we have to him are enough to show that a small share of paternal affection fell to his lot. "Have you heard any lessons from your father different from what we have all heard?" asked an inquisitive disciple of him. "No," replied Le, "he was standing alone once when I was passing through the court below with hasty steps, and said to me, 'Have you read the Odes?' On my replying, 'Not yet,' he added, 'If you do not learn the Odes, you will not be fit to converse with.' Another day, in the same place and the same way, he said to me, 'Have you read the rules of Propriety?' On my replying, 'Not yet,' he added, 'If you do not learn the rules of Propriety, your character cannot be established.'" "I asked one thing," said the enthusiastic disciple, "and I have learned three things. I have learnt about the Odes; I have learnt about the rules of Propriety; and I have learnt that the superior man maintains a distant reserve towards his son."

At the age of twenty-two we find Confucius released from the toils of office, and devoting his time to the more congenial task of imparting instruction to a band of admiring and earnest students. With idle or stupid scholars he would have nothing to do. "I do not open the truth," he said, "to one who is not eager after knowledge, nor do I help any one who is not anxious to explain himself. When I have presented one corner of a subject, and the listener cannot from it learn the other three, I do not repeat my lesson."

When twenty-eight years old Confucius studied archery, and in the following years took lessons in music from the celebrated master, Seang. At thirty he tells us "he stood firm," and about this time his fame mightily increased, many noble youths enrolled themselves among his disciples; and on his expressing a desire to visit the Imperial Court of Chow to confer on the subject of ancient ceremonies with Laou Tan, the founder of the Taouist sect, the reigning duke placed a carriage and horses at his disposal for the journey.

The extreme veneration which Confucius entertained for the founders of the Chow dynasty made the visit to Lŏ, the capital, one of intense interest to him. With eager delight he wandered through the temple and audience-chambers, the place of sacrifices and the palace, and having completed his inspection of the position and shape of the various sacrificial and ceremonial vessels, he turned to his disciples and said, "Now I understand the wisdom of the duke of Chow, and how his house attained to Imperial sway." But the principal object of his visit to Chow was to confer with Laou-tsze ; and of the interview between these two very dissimilar men we have various accounts. The Confucian writers as a rule merely mention the fact of their having met, but the admirers of Laou-tsze affirm that Confucius was very roughly handled by his more ascetic contemporary, who looked down from his somewhat higher standpoint with contempt on the great apostle of antiquity. It was only natural that Laou-tsze, who preached that stillness and self-emptiness were the highest attainable objects, should be ready to assail a man whose whole being was wrapt up in ceremonial observances and conscious well-doing. The very measured tones and considered movements of Confucius, coupled with a certain admixture of that pride which apes humility, must have been very irritating to the metaphysically-minded treasurer. And it was eminently characteristic of Confucius, that notwithstanding the great provocation given him on this occasion, he abstained from any rejoinder. We nowhere read of his engaging in a dispute. When an opponent arose, it was in keeping with the doctrine of Confucius to retire before him. "A sage," he said, "will not enter a tottering state nor dwell in a disorganized one. When right principles of government prevail he shows himself, but when they are prostrated he remains concealed." And carrying out the same principle in private life, he invariably refused to wrangle.

It was possibly in connection with this incident that Confucius drew the attention of his disciples to the metal statue of a man with a triple clasp upon his mouth, which stood in the ancestral temple at Lŏ. On the back of the statue were inscribed these words : " The ancients were guarded in their speech, and like them we should avoid loquacity. Many words invite many defeats. Avoid also engaging in many businesses, for many businesses create many difficulties." " Observe this, my children," said he, pointing to the inscription. " These words are true, and commend themselves to our reason."

Having gained all the information he desired in Chow, he returned to Loo, where pupils flocked to him until, we are told, he was surrounded by an admiring company of three thousand disciples. His stay in Loo was, however, of short duration, for the three principal clans of the state, those of Ke, Shŭh, and Mang, after frequent contests between themselves, engaged in a war with the reigning duke, and overthrew his armies. Upon this the duke took refuge in the state of T'se, whither Confucius followed him. As he passed along the road he saw a woman weeping at a tomb, and having compassion on her, he sent his disciple Tsze-loo to ask her the cause of her grief. "You weep as if you had experienced sorrow upon sorrow," said Tsze-loo. "I have," said the woman, "my father-in-law was killed here by a tiger, and my husband also ; and now my son has met the same fate." "Why, then, do you not remove from the place ?" asked Confucius. "Because here there is no oppressive government," replied the woman. On hearing this answer, Confucius remarked to his disciples, "My children remember this, oppressive government is fiercer than a tiger."

Possibly Confucius was attracted to T'se by a knowledge that the music of the emperor Shun was still preserved at the court. At all events, we are told that having heard a strain of the much-desired music on his way to the capital, he hurried on, and was so ravished with the airs he heard that for three months he never tasted flesh. "I did not think," said he, "that music could reach such a pitch of excellence."

Hearing of the arrival of the Sage, the Duke of T'se, King by name, sent for him, and after some conversation, being minded to act the part of a patron to so distinguished a visitor, offered to make him a present of the city of Lin-k'ew with its revenues. But this Confucius declined, remarking to his disciples, "A superior man will not receive rewards except for services done. I have given advice to the duke King, but he has not followed it as yet, and now he would endow me with this place. Very far is he from understanding me." He still, however, discussed politics with the duke, and taught him that, "There is good government when the prince is prince, and the minister is minister; when the father is father, and the son is son." "Good," said the duke; "if, indeed, the prince be not prince, the minister not minister, and the son not son, although I have my revenue, can I enjoy it?"

Though duke King was by no means a satisfactory pupil, many of his instincts were good, and he once again expressed a desire to pension Confucius, that he might keep him at hand; but Gan Ying, the Prime Minister, dissuaded him from his purpose. "These scholars," said the minister, "are impracticable, and cannot be imitated. They are haughty and conceited of their own views, so that they will not rest satisfied in inferior positions. They set a high value on all funeral ceremonies, give way to their grief, and will waste their property on great funerals, so that they would only be injurious to the common manners. This Kung Footsze has a thousand peculiarities. It would take ages to exhaust all he knows about the ceremonies of going up and going down. This is not the time to examine into his rules of propriety. If you wish to employ him to change the customs of T'se, you will not be making the people your primary consideration." This reasoning had full weight with the duke, who the next time he was urged to follow the advice of Confucius, cut short the discussion by the remark, " I am too old to adopt his doctrines."

Under these circumstances Confucius once more returned to Loo, only however to find that the condition of the State was still unchanged; disorder was rife; and the reins of government were in the hands of the head of the strongest party for the time being. This was no time for Confucius to take office, and he devoted the leisure thus forced upon him to the compilation of the " Book of Odes " and the " Book of History."

But in process of time order was once more restored, and he then felt himself free to accept the post of magistrate of the town of Chung-too, which was offered him by the duke Ting.

He now had an opportunity of putting his principles of government to the test, and the result partly justified his expectations. He framed rules for the support of the living, and for the observation of rites for the dead; he arranged appropriate food for the old and the young ; and he provided for the proper separation of men and women. And the results were, we are told, that, as in the time of king Alfred, a thing dropt on the road was not picked up ; there was no fraudulent carving of vessels ; coffins were made of the ordained thickness; graves were unmarked by mounds raised over them ; and no two prices were charged in the markets. The duke, surprised at what he saw, asked the sage whether his rule of government could be applied to the whole State. "Certainly," replied Confucius, " and not only to the state of Loo, but to the whole empire." Forthwith, therefore, the duke made him Assistant-Superintendent of Works, and shortly afterwards appointed him Minister of Crime.

Here, again, his success was complete. From the day of his appointment crime is said to have disappeared, and the penal laws remained a dead letter.

Courage was recognized by Confucius as being one of the great virtues, and about this period we have related two instances in which he showed that he possessed both moral and physical courage to a high degree. The chief of the Ke family, being virtual possessor of the State, when the body of the exiled duke Chaou was brought from T'se for interment, directed that it should be buried apart from the graves of his ancestors. On Confucius becoming aware of this decision, he ordered a trench to be dug round the burying-ground which should enclose the new tomb. "Thus to censure a prince and signalize his faults is not according to etiquette," said he to Ke. "I have caused the grave to be included in the cemetery, and I have done so to hide your disloyalty." And his action was allowed to pass unchallenged.

The other instance referred to was on the occasion, a few years later, of an interview between the dukes of Loo and T'se, at which Confucius was present as master of ceremonies. At his instigation an altar was raised at the place of meeting, which was mounted by three steps, and on this the dukes ascended, and having pledged one another proceeded to discuss a treaty of alliance. But treachery was intended on the part of the duke of T'se, and at a given signal a band of savages advanced with beat of drum to carry off the duke of Loo. Some such stratagem had been considered probable by Confucius, and the instant

the danger became imminent he rushed to the altar
and led away the duke. After much disorder, in
which Confucius took a firm and prominent part, a
treaty was concluded, and even some land on the
south of the river Wăn, which had been taken by
Ts'e, was by the exertions of the Sage restored to
Loo. On this recovered territory the people of Loo,
in memory of the circumstance, built a city and called
it, " The City of Confession."

But to return to Confucius as the Minister of
Crime. Though eminently successful, the results obtained under his system were not quite such as his
followers have represented them to have been. No
doubt crime diminished under his rule, but it was by
no means abolished. In fact, his biographers mention a case which must have been peculiarly shocking
to him. A father brought an accusation against his
son, in the expectation, probably, of gaining his suit
with ease before a judge who laid such stress on the
virtues of filial piety. But to his surprise, and that of
the on-lookers, Confucius cast both father and son into
prison, and to the remonstrances of the head of the
Ke clan answered, "Am I to punish for a breach of
filial piety one who has never been taught to be
filially minded? Is not he who neglects to teach his
son his duties, equally guilty with the son who fails
in them? Crime is not inherent in human nature,
and therefore the father in the family and the government in the State are responsible for the crimes committed against filial piety and the public laws. If a
king is careless about publishing laws, and then
peremptorily punishes in accordance with the strict

letter of them, he acts the part of a swindler; if he collect the taxes arbitrarily without giving warning, he is guilty of oppression; and if he puts the people to death without having instructed them, he commits a cruelty."

On all these points Confucius frequently insisted, and strove both by precept and example to impart the spirit they reflected on all around him. In the presence of his prince we are told that his manner, though self-possessed, displayed respectful uneasiness. When he entered the palace, or when he passed the vacant throne, his countenance changed, his legs bent under him, and he spoke as though he had scarcely breath to utter a word. When it fell to his lot to carry the royal sceptre, he stooped his body as though he were not able to bear its weight. If the prince came to visit him when he was ill, he had himself placed with his head to the east, and lay dressed in his court clothes with his girdle across them. When the prince sent him a present of cooked meat, he carefully adjusted his mat and just tasted the dishes; if the meat were uncooked, he offered it to the spirits of his ancestors, and any animal which was thus sent him he kept alive.

At the village festivals he never preceded, but always followed after the elders. To all about him he assumed an appearance of simplicity and sincerity. To the court officials of the lower grade he spoke freely, and to superior officers his manner was bland but precise. Even at the wild gatherings which accompanied the annual ceremony of driving away pestilential influences, he paid honour to the original meaning of the rite, by standing in court robes on the eastern steps of his house, and received the riotous exorcists as though they were favoured guests. When sent for by the prince to assist in receiving a royal visitor, his countenance appeared to change. He inclined himself to the officers among whom he stood, and when sent to meet the visitor at the gate, " he hastened forward with his arms spread out like the wings of a bird." Recognizing in the wind and the storm the voice of Heaven, he changed countenance at the sound of a sudden clap of thunder or a violent gust of wind.

The principles which underlie all these details relieve them from the sense of affected formality which they would otherwise suggest. Like the Sages of old, Confucius had an overweening faith in the effect of example. "What do you say," asked the chief of the Ke clan on one occasion, " to killing the unprincipled for the good of the principled?" "Sir," replied Confucius, "in carrying on your government why should you employ capital punishment at all? Let your evinced desires be for what is good, and the people will be good." And then quoting the words of King Ching, he added, " The relation between superiors and inferiors is like that between the wind and the grass. The grass must bend when the wind blows across it." Thus in every act of his life, whether at home or abroad, whether at table or in bed, whether at study or in moments of relaxation, he did all with the avowed object of being seen of men and of influencing them by his conduct. And to a certain extent he gained his end. He succeeded in demolishing a number of fortified cities which had formed the hotbeds of sedition and tumult; and thus added greatly to the power of the reigning duke. He inspired the men with a spirit of loyalty and good faith, and taught the women to be chaste and docile. On the report of the tranquillity prevailing in Loo, strangers flocked into the state, and thus was fulfilled the old criterion of good government which was afterwards repeated by Confucius, " the people were happy, and strangers were attracted from afar."

But even Confucius found it impossible to carry all his theories into practice, and his experience as Minister of Crime taught him that something more than mere example was necessary to lead the people into the paths of virtue. Before he had been many months in office, he signed the death-warrant of a well-known citizen named Shaou for disturbing the public peace. This departure from the principle he had so lately laid down astonished his followers, and Tszekung—the Simon Peter as he has been called among his disciples—took him to task for executing so notable a man. But Confucius held to it that the step was necessary. " There are five great evils in the world," said he : "a man with a rebellious heart who becomes dangerous ; a man who joins to vicious deeds a fierce temper ; a man whose words are knowingly false; a man who treasures in his memory noxious deeds and disseminates them ; a man who follows evil and fertilizes it. All these evil qualities were combined in Shaou. His house was a rendezvous for the disaffected ; his words were specious enough to dazzle any one ; and his opposition was violent enough to overthrow any independent man."

But notwithstanding such departures from the lines he had laid down for himself, the people gloried in his rule and sang at their work songs in which he was described as their saviour from oppression and wrong.

Confucius was an enthusiast, and his want of success in his attempt completely to reform the age in which he lived never seemed to suggest a doubt to his mind of the complete wisdom of his creed. According to his theory, his official administration should have effected the reform not only of his sovereign and the people, but of those of the neighbouring states. But what was the practical result? The contentment which reigned among the people of Loo, instead of instigating the Duke of Ts'e to institute a similar system, only served to rouse his jealousy. "With Confucius at the head of its government," said he, "Loo will become supreme among the states, and Ts'e, which is nearest to it, will be swallowed up. Let us propitiate it by a surrender of territory." But a more provident statesman suggested that they should first try to bring about the disgrace of the Sage.

With this object he sent eighty beautiful girls, well skilled in the arts of music and dancing, and a hundred and twenty of the finest horses which could be procured, as a present to the Duke Ting. The result fully realized the anticipation of the minister. The girls were taken into the duke's hareem, the horses were removed to the ducal stables, and Confucius was left to meditate on the folly of men who preferred listening to the songs of the maidens of Ts'e to the wisdom of Yaou and Shun. Day after day passed and the duke showed no signs of returning to his proper mind. The affairs of state were neglected, and for three days the duke refused to receive his ministers in audience.

"Master," said Tsze-loo, "it is time you went." But Confucius, who had more at stake than his disciple, was disinclined to give up the experiment on which his heart was set. Besides, the time was approaching when the great sacrifice to Heaven at the solstice, about which he had had so many conversations with the duke, should be offered up, and he hoped that the recollection of his weighty words would recall the duke to a sense of his duties. But his gay rivals in the affections of the duke still held their sway, and the recurrence of the great festival failed to awaken his conscience even for the moment. Reluctantly therefore Confucius resigned his post and left the capital.

But though thus disappointed of the hopes he entertained of the Duke of Loo, Confucius was by no means disposed to resign his *rôle* as the reformer of the age. "If any one among the princes would employ me," said he, "I would effect something considerable in the course of twelve months, and in three years the government would be perfected." But the tendencies of the times were unfavourable to the Sage. The struggle for supremacy which had been going on for centuries between the princes of the various states was then at its height, and though there might be a question whether it would finally result in the victory of Tsin, or of Ts'oo, or of Ts'in, there could be no doubt that the sceptre had already passed from the hands of the ruler of Chow. To men therefore who were fighting over the possessions of a state which had ceased to live, the idea of employing a minister whose principal object would have been to breathe life into the dead bones of Chow, was ridiculous. This soon became apparent to his disciples, who being even more concerned than their master at his loss of office, and not taking so exalted a view as he did of what he considered to be a heaven-sent mission, were inclined to urge him to make concessions in harmony with the times. "Your principles," said Tsze-kung to him, "are excellent, but they are unacceptable in the Empire, would it not be well therefore to bate them a little?" "A good husbandman," replied the Sage, "can sow, but he cannot secure a harvest. An artisan may excel in handicraft, but he cannot provide a market for his goods. And in the same way a superior man can cultivate his principles, but he cannot make them acceptable."

But Confucius was at least determined that no efforts on his part should be wanting to discover the opening for which he longed, and on leaving Loo he betook himself to the state of Wei. On arriving at the capital, the reigning duke received him with distinction, but showed no desire to employ him. Probably expecting however to gain some advantage from the counsels of the Sage in the art of governing, he determined to attach him to his court by the grant of an annual stipend of 60,000 measures of grain,—that having been the value of the post he had just resigned in Loo. Had the experiences of his public life come up to the sanguine hopes he had entertained at its beginning, Confucius would probably have declined . this offer as he did that of the Duke of Ts'e some years before, but poverty unconsciously impelled him to act up to the advice of Tsze-kung and to bate his principles of conduct somewhat. His stay, however, in Wei was of short duration. The officials at the court, jealous probably of the influence they feared he might gain over the duke, intrigued against him, and Confucius thought it best to bow before the coming storm. After living on the duke's hospitality for ten months, he left the capital, intending to visit the state of Ch'in.

It chanced, however, that the way thither led him through the town of Kwang, which had suffered much from the filibustering expeditions of a notorious disturber of the public peace, named Yang Hoo. To this man of ill-fame Confucius bore a striking resemblance, so much so that the townspeople, fancying that they now had their old enemy in their power, surrounded the house in which he lodged for five days, intending to attack him. The situation was certainly disquieting, and the disciples were much alarmed. But Confucius's belief in the heaven-sent nature of his mission raised him above fear. "After the death of King Wăn," said he, "was not the cause of truth lodged in me? If Heaven had wished to let this sacred cause perish, I should not have been put into such a relation to it. Heaven will not let the cause of truth perish, and what therefore can the people of

Kwang do to me ?" Saying which he tuned his lyre, and sang probably some of those songs from his recently compiled Book of Odes which breathed the wisdom of the ancient emperors.

From some unexplained cause, but more probably from the people of Kwang discovering their mistake than from any effect produced by Confucius's ditties, the attacking force suddenly withdrew, leaving the Sage free to go wherever he listed. This misadventure was sufficient to deter him from wandering further a-field, and, after a short stay at Poo, he returned to Wei. Again the duke welcomed him to the capital, though it does not appear that he renewed his stipend, and even his consort Nan-tsze forgot for a while her intrigues and debaucheries at the news of his arrival. With a complimentary message she begged an interview with the Sage, which he at first refused; but on her urging her request, he was fain obliged to yield the point. On being introduced into her presence, he found her concealed behind a screen, in strict accordance with the prescribed etiquette, and after the usual formalities they entered freely into conversation.

Tsze-loo was much disturbed at this want of discretion, as he considered it, on the part of Confucius, and the vehemence of his master's answer showed that there was a doubt in his own mind whether he had not overstepped the limits of sage-like propriety. "Wherein I have done improperly," said he, "may Heaven reject me! may Heaven reject me!" This incident did not, however, prevent him from maintaining friendly relations with the court, and it was

not until the duke by a public act showed his in-
ability to understand the dignity of the rôle which
Confucius desired to assume, that he lost all hope of
finding employment in the state of his former patron.
On this occasion the duke drove through the streets
of his capital seated in a carriage with Nan-tsze, and
desired Confucius to follow in a carriage behind.
As the procession passed through the market-place,
the people perceiving more clearly than the duke the
incongruity of the proceeding, laughed and jeered at
the idea of making virtue follow in the wake of lust.
This completed the shame which Confucius felt at
being in so false a position. "I have not seen one,"
said he, "who loves virtue as he loves beauty." To
stay any longer under the protection of a court which
could inflict such an indignity upon him was more
than he could do, and he therefore once again struck
southward towards Ch'in.

After his retirement from office it is probable that
Confucius devoted himself afresh to imparting to his
followers those doctrines and opinions which we shall
consider later on. Even on the road to Ch'in we
are told that he practised ceremonies with his disciples beneath the shadow of a tree by the wayside in
Sung. In the spirit of Laou-tsze, Hwuy T'uy, an
officer in the neighbourhood, was angered at his
reported " proud air and many desires, his insinuating
habit and wild will," and attempted to prevent him
entering the state. In this endeavour, however, he
was unsuccessful, as were some more determined
opponents, who two years later attacked him at Poo,
when he was on his way to Wei. On this occasion

he was seized, and though it is said that his followers struggled manfully with his captors, their efforts did not save him from having to give an oath that he would not continue his journey to Wei. But in spite of his oath, and in spite of the public slight which had previously been put upon him by the Duke of Wei, an irresistible attraction drew him towards that state, and he had no sooner escaped from the clutches of his captors than he continued his journey.

This deliberate forfeiture of his word in one who had commanded them to "hold faithfulness and sincerity as first principles," surprised his disciples; and Tsze-kung, who was generally the spokesman on such occasions, asked him whether it was right to violate the oath he had taken. But Confucius, who had learned expediency in adversity, replied, "It was an oath extracted by force. The spirits do not hear such."

But to return to Confucius flying from his enemies in Sung. Finding his way barred by the action of Hwan T'uy, he proceeded westward and arrived at Ch'ing, the capital of the state of the same name. Thither it would appear his disciples had preceded him, and he arrived unattended at the eastern gate of the city. But his appearance was so striking that his followers were soon made aware of his presence. "There is a man," said a townsman to Tsze-kung, "standing at the east gate with a forehead like Yaou, a neck like Kaou Yaou, his shoulders on a level with those of Tsze-ch'an, but wanting below the waist three inches of the height of Yu, and altogether having the forsaken appearance of a stray dog." Recognizing

his master in this description, Tsze-kung hastened
to meet him, and repeated to him the words of his
informant.   Confucius was much amused, and said :
" The personal appearance is a small matter ; but to
say I was like a stray dog—capital ! capital !"

The ruling powers in Ch'ing, however, showed
no disposition to employ even a man possessing
such marked characteristics, and before long he
removed to Ch'in, where he remained a year.
From Ch'in he once more turned his face towards
Wei, and it was while he was on this journey
that he was detained at P'oo, as mentioned above.
Between Confucius and the Duke of Wei there evidently existed a personal liking, if not friendship.
The duke was always glad to see him and ready to
converse with him ; but Confucius's unbounded admiration for those whose bones, as Laou-tsze said,
were mouldered to dust, and especially for the founders
of the Chow dynasty, made it impossible for the duke
to place him in any post of importance.   At the same
time Confucius seems always to have hoped that he
would be able to gain the duke over to his views ;
and thus it came about that the Sage was constantly
attracted to the court of Duke Ling, and as often
compelled to exile himself from it.

On this particular occasion, as at all other times, the
duke received him gladly, but their conversations,
which had principally turned on the act of peaceful
government, were now directed to warlike affairs.
The duke was contemplating an attack on P'oo, the
inhabitants of which, under the leadership of Hwan
T'uy, who had arrested Confucius, had rebelled

against him. At first Confucius was quite disposed to support the duke in his intended hostilities; but a representation from the duke that the probable support of other states would make the expedition one of considerable danger, converted Confucius to the opinion evidently entertained by the duke, that it would be best to leave Hwan T'uy in possession of his ill-gotten territory. Confucius's latest advice was then to this effect, and the duke acted upon it.

The duke was now becoming an old man, and with advancing age came a disposition to leave the task of governing to others, and to weary of Confucius's high-flown lectures. He ceased "to use" Confucius, as the Chinese historians say, and the Sage was therefore indignant, and ready to accept any offer which might come from any quarter. While in this humour he received an invitation from Pih Hih, an officer of the state of Tsin who was holding the town of Chung-mow against his chief, to visit him, and he was inclined to go. It is impossible to study this portion of Confucius's career without feeling that a great change had come over his conduct. There was no longer that lofty love of truth and of virtue which had distinguished the commencement of his official life. Adversity, instead of stiffening his back, had made him pliable. He who had formerly refused to receive money he had not earned, was now willing to take pay in return for no other services than the presentation of courtier-like advice on occasions when Duke Ling desired to have his opinion in support of his own; and in defiance of his oft-repeated denunciation of rebels, he was now ready to go over to the court of a rebel chief, in the hope possibly of being able through his means "to establish," as he said on another occasion, "an Eastern Chow."

Again Tsze-loo interfered, and expostulated with him on his inconsistency. "Master," said he, "I have heard you say that when a man is guilty of personal wrong-doing, a superior man will not associate with him. If you accept the invitation of this Pih Hih, who is in open rebellion against his chief, what will people say?" But Confucius, with a dexterity which had now become common with him, replied: "It is true I have said so. But is it not also true that if a thing be really hard, it may be ground without being made thin; and if it be really white, it may be steeped in a black fluid without becoming black? Am I a bitter gourd? Am I to be hung up out of the way of being eaten." But nevertheless Tsze-loo's remonstrances prevailed, and he did not go.

His relations with the duke did not improve, and so dissatisfied was he with his patron that he retired from the court. As at this time Confucius was not in the receipt of any official income, it is probable that he again provided for his wants by imparting to his disciples some of the treasures out of the rich stores of learning which he had collected by means of diligent study and of a wide experience. Every word and action of Confucius were full of such meaning to his admiring followers that they have enabled us to trace him into the retirement of private life. In his dress, we are told, he was careful to wear only the "correct" colours, viz. azure, yellow, carnation, white and black, and he scrupulously avoided red as being the colour usually affected by women and girls. At the table he was moderate in his appetite but particular as to the nature of his food and the manner in which it was set before him. Nothing would induce him to touch any meat that was "high" or rice that was musty, nor would he eat anything that was not properly cut up or accompanied with the proper sauce. He allowed himself only a certain quantity of meat and rice, and though no such limit was fixed to the amount of wine with which he accompanied his frugal fare, we are assured that he never allowed himself to be confused by it. When out driving, he never turned his head quite round, and in his actions as well as in his words he avoided all appearance of haste.

Such details are interesting in the case of a man like Confucius, who has exercised so powerful an influence over so large a proportion of the world's inhabitants, and whose instructions, far from being confined to the courts of kings, found their loudest utterances in intimate communings with his disciples, and in the example he set by the exact performance of his daily duties.

The only accomplishment which Confucius possessed was a love of music, and this he studied less as an accomplishment than as a necessary part of education. "It is by the odes that the mind is aroused," said he. "It is by the rules of propriety that the character is established. And it is music which completes the edifice."

But having tasted the sweets of official life, Confucius was not inclined to resign all hope of future employment, and the Duke of Wei still remaining deaf to his advice, he determined to visit the state of Tsin, in the hope of finding in Chaou Keen-tsze, one of the three chieftains who virtually governed that state, a more hopeful pupil. With this intention he started westward, but had got no further than the Yellow River when the news reached him of the execution of Tuh Ming and Tuh Shun-hwa, two men of note in Tsin. The disorder which this indicated put a stop to his journey; for had not he himself said " that a superior man will not enter a tottering state." His disappointment and grief were great, and looking at the yellow waters as they flowed at his feet, he sighed and muttered to himself : " Oh how beautiful were they ; this river is not more majestic than they were ! and I was not there to avert their fate ! "

So saying he returned to Wei, only to find the duke as little inclined to listen to his lectures, as he was deeply engaged in warlike preparations. When Confucius presented himself at court, the duke refused to talk on any other subject but military tactics, and forgetting, possibly on purpose, that Confucius was essentially a man of peace, pressed him for information on the art of manoeuvring an army. " If you should wish to know how to arrange sacrificial vessels," said the Sage, " I will answer you, but about warfare I know nothing."

Confucius was now sixty years old, and the condition of the states composing the empire was even more unfavourable for the reception of his doctrines than ever. But though depressed by fortune, he never lost that steady confidence in himself and his mission, which was a leading characteristic of his career, and

E

when he found the Duke of Wei deaf to his advice, he removed to Ch'in, in the hope of there finding a ruler who would appreciate his wisdom.

In the following year he left Ch'in with his disciples for Ts'ae, a small dependency of the state of Ts'oo. In those days the empire was subjected to constant changes. One day a new state carved out of an old one would appear, and again it would disappear, or increase in size, as the fortunes of war might determine. Thus while Confucius was in Ts'ae, a part of Ts'oo declared itself independent, under the name of Yĕ, and the ruler usurped the title of duke. In earlier days such rebellion would have called forth a rebuke from Confucius ; but it was otherwise now, and, instead of denouncing the usurper as a rebel, he sought him as a patron. The duke did not know how to receive his visitor, and asked Tsze-loo about him. But Tsze-loo, possibly because he considered the duke to be no better than Pih Hih, returned him no answer. For this reticence Confucius found fault with him, and said, " Why did you not say to him, ' He is simply a man who, in his eager pursuit of knowledge, forgets his food ; who, in the joy of its attainments, forgets his sorrows ; and who does not perceive that old age is coming on ? ' "

But whatever may have been the opinion of Tsze-loo, Confucius was quite ready to be on friendly terms with the duke, who seems to have had no keener relish for Confucius's ethics than the other rulers to whom he had offered his services. We are only told of one conversation which took place between the duke and the Sage, and on that occasion the duke questioned him on the subject of government. Confucius's reply was eminently characteristic of the man. Most of his definitions of good government would have sounded unpleasantly in the ears of a man who had just thrown off his master's yoke and headed a successful rebellion, so he cast about for one which might offer some excuse for the new duke by attributing the fact of his disloyalty to the bad government of his late ruler. Quoting the words of an earlier sage, he replied, "Good government obtains when those who are near are made happy, and those who are far off are attracted."

Returning from Yĕ to Ts'ae, he came to a river which, being unbridged, left him no resource but to ford it. Seeing two men whom he recognized as political recluses ploughing in a neighbouring field, he sent the ever-present Tsze-loo to inquire of them where best he could effect a crossing. "Who is that holding the reins in the carriage yonder?" asked the first addressed, in answer to Tsze-loo's inquiry. "Kung Kew," replied the disciple. "Kung Kew, of Loo?" asked the ploughman. "Yes," was the reply. "*He* knows the ford," was the enigmatic answer of the man as he turned again to his work; but whether this reply was suggested by the general belief that Confucius was omniscient, or by way of a parable to signify that Confucius possessed the knowledge by which the river of disorder, which was barring the progress of liberty and freedom, might be crossed, we are only left to conjecture. Nor from the second recluse could Tsze-loo gain any practical information. "Who are you, sir?" was the somewhat peremptory question which his inquiry met with. Upon his answering that he was a disciple of Confucius, the man, who might have gathered his estimate of Confucius from the mouth of Laou-tsze, replied : " Disorder, like a swelling flood, spreads over the whole empire, and who is he who will change it for you ? Rather than follow one who merely withdraws from this court to that court, had you not better follow those who (like ourselves) withdraw from the world altogether ?" These words Tsze-loo, as was his wont, repeated to Confucius, who thus justified his career : " It is impossible to associate with birds and beasts as if they were the same as ourselves. If I associate not with people, with mankind, with whom shall I associate ? If right principles prevailed throughout the empire, there would be no necessity for me to change its state."

Altogether Confucius remained three years in Ts'ae,—three years of strife and war, during which his counsels were completely neglected. Towards their close, the state of Woo made an attack on Ch'in, which found support from the powerful state of Ts'oo on the south. While thus helping his ally, the Duke of Ts'oo heard that Confucius was in Ts'ae, and determined to invite him to his court. With this object he sent messengers bearing presents to the Sage, and charged them with a message begging him to come to Ts'oo. Confucius readily accepted the invitation, and prepared to start. But the news of the transaction alarmed the ministers of Ts'ae and Ch'in. " Ts'oo," said they, " is already a powerful state, and Confucius is a man of wisdom. Experience has proved that those who have despised him have invariably suffered for it, and, should he succeed in guiding the affairs of Ts'oo, we should certainly be ruined. At all hazards we must stop his going." When, therefore, Confucius had started on his journey, these men despatched a force which hemmed him in in a wild bit of desert country. Here, we are told, they kept him a prisoner for seven days, during which time he suffered severe privations, and, as was always the case in moments of difficulty, the disciples loudly bewailed their lot and that of their master.

"Has the superior man," said Tsze-loo, "indeed, to endure in this way?" "The superior man may indeed have to suffer want," replied Confucius, "but it is only the mean man who, when he is in straits, gives way to unbridled license." In this emergency he had recourse to a solace which had soothed him on many occasions when fortune frowned : he played on his lute and sang.

At length he succeeded in sending word to the Duke of Ts'oo of the position he was in. At once the duke sent ambassadors to liberate him, and he himself went out of his capital to meet him. But though he welcomed him cordially, and seems to have availed himself of his advice on occasions, he did not appoint him to any office, and the intention he at one time entertained of granting him a slice of territory was thwarted by his ministers, from motives of expediency. "Has your majesty," said this officer, "any servant who could discharge the duties of ambassador like Tsze-kung? or any one so well qualified for a premier as Yen Hwuy? or any one to compare as a general with Tsze-loo? Did not kings

Wăn and Woo, from their small states of Fung and Kaou, rise to the sovereignty of the empire? And if K'ung K'ew once acquired territory, with such disciples to be his ministers, it will not be to the prosperity of Ts'oo."

This remonstrance not only had the immediate effect which was intended, but appears to have influenced the manner of the duke towards the Sage, for in the interval between this and the duke's death, in the autumn of the same year, we hear of no counsel being either asked or given. In the successor to the throne Confucius evidently despaired of finding a patron, and he once again returned to Wei.

Confucius was now sixty-three, and on arriving at Wei he found a grandson of his former friend, the Duke Ling, holding the throne against his own father, who had been driven into exile for attempting the life of his mother, the notorious Nan-tsze. This chief, who called himself the Duke Chuh, being conscious how much his cause would be strengthened by the support of Confucius, sent Tsze-loo to him, saying, "The Prince of Wei has been waiting to secure your services in the administration of the state, and wishes to know what you consider is the first thing to be done." "It is first of all necessary," replied Confucius, "to rectify names." "Indeed," said Tzse-loo, "you are wide of the mark. Why need there be such rectification?" "How uncultivated you are, Yew," answered Confucius; "a superior man shows a cautious reserve in regard to what he does not know. If names be not correct, language is not in accordance with the truth of things. If language be not in accordance with the truth of things, affairs cannot be carried on successfully. When affairs cannot be carried on successfully, proprieties and music will not flourish. When proprieties and music do not flourish, punishments will not properly be awarded. When punishments are not properly awarded, the people do not know how to move hand or foot. Therefore the superior man considers it necessary that names should be used appropriately, and that his directions should be carried out appropriately. A superior man requires that his words should be correct."

The position of things in Wei was naturally such as Confucius could not sanction, and, as the duke showed no disposition to amend his ways, the Sage left his court, and lived the remainder of the five or six years, during which he sojourned in the state, in close retirement.

He had now been absent from his native state of Loo for fourteen years, and the time had come when he was to return to it. But, by the irony of fate, the accomplishment of his long-felt desire was due, not to his reputation for political or ethical wisdom, but to his knowledge of military tactics, which he heartily despised. It happened that at this time Yen Yew, a disciple of the Sage, being in the service of Ke K'ang, conducted a campaign against Ts'e with much success. On his triumphal return, Ke K'ang asked him how he had acquired his military skill. "From Confucius," replied the general. "And what kind of man is he?" asked Ke K'ang. "Were you to employ him," answered Yen Yew, "your fame would spread abroad; your people might face demons and gods, and would have nothing either to fear or to ask of them. And if you accepted his principles, were you to collect a thousand altars of the spirits of the land it would profit you nothing." Attracted by such a prospect, Ke K'ang proposed to invite the Sage to his court. "If you do," said Yen Yew, "mind you do not allow mean men to come between you and him."

But before Ke K'ang's invitation reached Confucius an incident occurred which made the arrival of the messengers from Loo still more welcome to him. K'ung Wăn, an officer of Wei, came to consult him as to the best means of attacking the force of another officer with whom he was engaged in a feud. Confucius, disgusted at being consulted on such a subject, professed ignorance, and prepared to leave the state, saying as he went away : " The bird chooses its tree ; the tree does not choose the bird." At this juncture Ke K'ang's envoys arrived, and without hesitation he accepted the invitation they brought. On arriving at Loo, he presented himself at court, and in reply to a question of the Duke Gae on the subject of government, threw out a strong hint that the duke might do well to offer him an appointment. "Government," he said, "consists in the right choice of ministers." To the same question put by Ke K'ang he replied, " Employ the upright and put aside the crooked, and thus will the crooked be made upright."

At this time Ke K'ang was perplexed how to deal with the prevailing brigandage. " If you, sir, were not avaricious, though you might offer rewards to induce people to steal, they would not." This answer sufficiently indicates the estimate formed by Confucius of Ke K'ang and therefore of the duke Gae, for so entirely were the two of one mind that the acts of Ke K'ang appear to have been invariably endorsed by the duke. It was plainly impossible that Confucius could serve under such a régime, and instead, therefore, of seeking employment, he retired to his study and devoted himself to the completion of his literary undertaking.

He was now sixty-nine years of age, and if a man is to be considered successful only when he succeeds in realizing the dream of his life, he must be deemed to have been unfortunate. Endowed by nature with a large share of reverence, a cold rather than a fervid disposition, and a studious mind, and reared in the traditions of the ancient kings, whose virtuous achievements obtained an undue prominence by the obliteration of all their faults and failures, he believed himself capable of effecting far more than it was possible for him or any other man to accomplish. In the earlier part of his career, he had in Loo an opportunity given him for carrying his theories of government into practice, and we have seen how they failed to do more than produce a temporary improvement in the condition of the people under his immediate rule. But he had a lofty and steady confidence in himself and in the principles which he professed, which prevented his accepting the only legitimate inference which could be drawn from his want of success. The lessons of his own experience were entirely lost upon him, and he went down to his grave at the age of seventy-two firmly convinced as of yore that if he were placed in a position of authority

" in three years the government would be perfected."

Finding it impossible to associate himself with the rulers of Loo, he appears to have resigned himself to exclusion from office. His wanderings were over—

> And as a hare, when hounds and horns pursue,
> Pants to the place from whence at first he flew,

he had lately been possessed with an absorbing desire to return once more to Loo. This had at last been brought about, and he made up his mind to spend the remainder of his days in his native state. He had now leisure to finish editing the Shoo King, or " Book of History," to which he wrote a preface ; he also " carefully digested the rites and ceremonies determined by the wisdom of the more ancient sages and kings; collected and arranged the ancient poetry; and undertook the reform of music." He made a diligent study of the " Book of Changes," and added a commentary to it, which is sufficient to show that the original meaning of the work was as much a mystery to him as it has been to others. His idea of what would probably be the value of the kernel encased in this unusually hard shell, if it were once rightly understood, is illustrated by his remark " that if some years could be added to his life, he would give fifty of them to the study of the Book of Changes, and that then he expected to be without great faults."

In the year 482 B.C. his son Le died, and in the following year he lost by death his faithful disciple Yen Hwuy. When the news of this last misfortune reached him, he exclaimed, "Alas! Heaven is destroying me !" A year later a servant of Ke K'ang caught a strange one-horned animal while on a hunting excursion, and as no one present could tell what animal it was, Confucius was sent for. At once he declared it to be a K'e-lin, and legend says that its identity with the one which appeared before his birth was proved by its having the piece of ribbon on its horn which Ching-tsae tied to the weird animal which presented itself to her in a dream on Mount Ne. This second apparition could only have one meaning, and Confucius was profoundly affected at the portent. "For whom have you come?" he cried, "for whom have you come?" and then, bursting into tears, he added, "The course of my doctrine is run, and I am unknown."

"How do you mean that you are unknown?" asked Tsze-kung. "I don't complain of Providence," answered the Sage, "nor find fault with men that learning is neglected and success is worshipped. Heaven knows me. . . . Never does a superior man pass away without leaving a name behind him. But my principles make no progress, and I, how shall I be viewed in future ages?"

At this time, notwithstanding his declining strength and his many employments, he wrote the "Ch'un ts'ew, or Spring and Autumn Annals," in which he followed the history of his native state of Loo, from the time of the Duke Yin to the fourteenth year of the Duke Gae, that is, to the time when the appearance of the K'e-lin warned him to consider his life at an end.

This is the only work of which Confucius was the

author, and of this every word is his own. His
biographers say that "what was written, he wrote, and
what was erased, was erased by him." Not an expression was either inserted or altered by any one
but himself. When he had completed the work, he
handed the manuscript to his disciples, saying, "By
the Spring and Autumn Annals I shall be known,
and by the Spring and Autumn Annals I shall be
condemned." This only furnishes another of the
many instances in which authors have entirely mis-
judged the value of their own works.

In the estimation of his countrymen even, whose
reverence for his every word would incline them to
accept his opinion on this as on every subject, the
Spring and Autumn Annals holds a very secondary
place, his utterances recorded in the *Lun yu*, or
" Confucian Analects," being esteemed of far higher
value, as they undoubtedly are. And indeed the
two works he compiled, the "Shoo king" and the "She
king," hold a very much higher place in the public
regard than the book on which he so prided himself.
To foreigners, whose judgments are unhampered by
his recorded opinion, his character as an original
historian sinks into insignificance, and he is known
only as a philosopher and statesman.

Once again only do we hear of Confucius presenting himself at the court of the duke after this.
And this was on the occasion of the murder of the
Duke of Ts'e by one of his officers. We must suppose that the crime was one of a gross nature, for it
raised Confucius's fiercest anger, and he who never
wearied of singing the praises of those virtuous men

who overthrew the thrones of licentious and tyrannous kings, would have had no room for blame if the murdered duke had been like unto Këë or Show. But the outrage was one which Confucius felt should be avenged, and he therefore bathed and presented himself at court.

"Sir," said he, addressing the duke, "Ch'in Hăng has slain his sovereign; I beg that you will undertake to punish him." But the duke was indisposed to move in the matter, and pleaded the comparative strength of Ts'e. Confucius, however, was not to be so silenced. "One half of the people of Ts'e," said he, "are not consenting to the deed. If you add to the people of Loo one half of the people of Ts'e, you will be sure to overcome." This numerical argument no more affected the duke than the statement of the fact, and wearying with Confucius's importunity, he told him to lay the matter before the chiefs of the three principal families of the state. Before this court of appeal, whither he went with reluctance, his cause fared no better, and the murder remained unavenged.

At a period when every prince held his throne by the strength of his right arm, revolutions lost half their crime, and must have been looked upon rather as trials of strength than as disloyal villanies. The frequency of their occurrence, also, made them less the subjects of surprise and horror. At the time of which we write, the states in the neighbourhood of Loo appear to have been in a very disturbed condition. Immediately following on the murder of the Duke of Ts'e, news was brought to Confucius that a revolution had broken out in Wei. This was an occurrence which particularly interested him, for when he returned from Wei to Loo he left Tsze-loo and Tsze-kaou, two of his disciples, engaged in the official service of the state. "Tsze-kaou will return," was Confucius's remark, when he was told of the outbreak, "but Tsze-loo will die." The prediction was verified. For when Tsze-kaou saw that matters were desperate he made his escape; but Tsze-loo remained to defend his chief, and fell, fighting in the cause of his master. Though Confucius had looked forward to the event as probable, he was none the less grieved when he heard that it had come about, and he mourned for his friend, whom he was so soon to follow to the grave.

One morning, in the spring of the year 478 B.C., he walked in front of his door, mumbling as he went :—

> The great mountain must crumble ;
> The strong beam must break ;
> And the wise man withers away like a plant.

These words came as a presage of evil to the faithful Tsze-kung. "If the great mountain crumble," said he, "to what shall I look up? If the strong beam break, and the wise man wither away, on whom shall I lean? The master, I fear, is going to be ill." So saying, he hastened after Confucius into the house. "What makes you so late?" said Confucius, when the disciple presented himself before him ; and then he added, "According to the statutes of Hea, the corpse was dressed and coffined at the top of the eastern steps, treating the dead as if he were still the host. Under the Yin, the ceremony was performed between the two pillars, as if the dead were both host and guest. The rule of Chow is to perform it at the top of the western steps, treating the dead as if he were a guest. I am a man of Yin, and last night I dreamt that I was sitting, with offerings before me, between the two pillars. No intelligent monarch arises ; there is not one in the empire who will make me his master. My time is come to die." It is eminently characteristic of Confucius that in his last recorded speech and dream, his thoughts should so have dwelt on the ceremonies of bygone ages. But the dream had its fulfilment. That same day he took to his bed, and after a week's illness he expired.

On the banks of the river Sze, to the north of the capital city of Loo, his disciples buried him, and for three years they mourned at his grave. Even such marked respect as this fell short of the homage which Tsze-kung, his most faithful disciple, felt was due to him, and for three additional years that loving follower testified by his grief his reverence for his master. " I have all my life had the heaven above my head," said he, " but I do not know its height; and the earth under my feet, but I know not its thickness. In serving Confucius, I am like a thirsty man, who goes with his pitcher to the river and there drinks his fill, without knowing the river's depth."

Mr. Williamson, who in 1865 visited the tomb of the Sage, thus describes it as it at present exists : " A fine avenue of old cypress-trees leads due north from the north gate to the burial-ground. In a forest of oak, cypress, and other trees, enclosed by a high wall, is the grave. Entering the graveyard, we passed through a finely ornamented gate, and then to a second avenue, with lions and other creatures in stone on either hand, and the unfailing cypress overhead. As we approached the tomb, two sages larger than life faced each other, looking most solemnly, as if they wished to remind the visitor of the sacredness of the place. Passing the house where sacrifices are prepared and the worshippers rest and meditate, we were shown a tree planted by Tsze-kung, one of the Sage's disciples, and a pavilion erected by the emperor Keen-lung. . . . . The tomb of Confucius is a huge mound, overgrown with trees and shrubs, having in front of it the usual arrangements for sacrifice. Beside it stands a tablet, twenty-five feet high by six feet broad, on which are engraved the name and doings of the Sage. . . . . On the west of the tomb of the Sage is that of his son Le . . . . and all around the graves of the chiefs of the clan."

The descriptions given by his contemporaries of the appearance of the Sage are so allegorical that they represent nothing definite to the mind, and pre-suppose an intimate acquaintance on the part of the reader with the outward form and shape of the emperors Yaou and Shun. In his name Kew we have reference to a peculiarity in the shape of his head, which is said to have resembled Mount Kew in having a hollow on the top; whence his name. His statue, which stands in the temple adjoining his tomb, represents him as having been " tall, strong, and well-built, with a full, red face, and large and heavy head."

CHAPTER III.

THE TEACHINGS OF CONFUCIUS.

POSTERITY is the truest judge of a man's work. Many things may tend to warp the judgment of his contemporaries. His adoption of the popular view of the politics of the day may raise him to an extravagant height in their estimation, or should the opposite party enlist his advocacy, he may be proportionately undervalued   No such considerations influence the finding of posterity.   Being removed by time from the passions of the day, they are removed also from its prejudices. They are not so much concerned with the struggles and throes of parties as with the results to which those struggles and throes give birth. To them the hero of an age appears not unfrequently as a charlatan ; and in their estimation the man of genius, depressed by fortune and borne down by adversity, is restored to his legitimate position.

No great character in history can appeal more surely from the opinion of his contemporaries to the verdict of posterity than Confucius. He was essentially a statesman, and the political views he advocated required for their development a sustained period of peace and quiet. He was born for a time of peace,

F

and he was nurtured amid the clash of arms ; he was designed by nature for the council-chamber, and he was destined to find governments administered by armed men surrounded by the din of war. The times were against him, and he was obliged to yield to the decrees of fate. Instead of being the honoured adviser of a virtuous sovereign striving to reproduce the heroic age of Yaou and Shun among a contented and law-abiding people, he spent the greater part of his life in offering his services to princes who disdained his overtures and laughed at his theories. It was a time of universal disorder and anarchy. " Right principles had long deserted the empire," and power had become the only standard of truth and virtue.

No wonder, then, that Confucius's career was a failure. He was not a man who could shamelessly trim his sails to the passing breeze, and for him to fail was to enter his protest against the iniquities of the time. But what was lost to his contemporaries has been preserved for posterity. To the succeeding millions of China it has been a matter of unimportance that he was excluded from the council-chambers of princes, so long as they have had access to the words of wisdom with which he instructed his disciples, and thus they have cared not for the contempt with which he was treated by lawless chiefs, so long as they have been able to make his views on the principles of government, and on the duties of citizens their own.

Probably no man has been so contemned during his lifetime, and at the same time so worshipped by posterity, as Confucius. In both extremes there has been some exaggeration. His standard of morality was high, and his doctrines were pure. Had he therefore had an opportunity of exercising authority, it can but have resulted in good to an age when the notions of right and wrong were strangely confused, and when both public and private morality were at the lowest ebb. On the other hand, it is difficult to understand the secret of the extraordinary influence he has gained over posterity, and the more the problem is studied the more incomprehensible does it become. His system of philosophy is by no means complete, and it lacks life, if we may venture to say so in face of the fact that it has supplied the guiding principles which have actuated the performance of all that is great and noble in the life of China for more than twenty centuries.

The Confucian literature as it stands at the present day is very large ; but if we separate out of the mass those canonical works which, according to universal belief, contain the complete system of Confucius, we shall hold in our hands only three thin volumes. The first is the *Lun Yu*, or "Confucian Analects," in which have been collected by the disciples the sayings of their great master. The other two are the *Ta Heŏ*, or "Great Learning," and the *Chung Yung*, or "Doctrine of the Mean," both of which have been very generally attributed to Tsze-sze, the grandson of Confucius, and both of which contain digests of the doctrines of the Sage. But Confucius was less of an original thinker than a "transmitter," as he calls himself, and therefore it becomes necessary to see what the older canonical works, such as the *Yih King*, or

" Book of Changes," the *She King*, or " Book of Odes," and the *Shoo King*, or " Book of History," say with regard to the subjects of which he treats. In so doing we shall see that Confucius did not transmit faithfully the doctrines of the ancient sages, but, being unable to understand the spiritual side of the characters of those for whom he professed such unbounded admiration, lowered their teachings to the inferior level which he occupied.

There is nothing spiritual in the teachings of Confucius. He rather avoided all references to the supernatural. In answer to a question about death, he answered, " While you do not know life, how do you know about death?" Life, then, was his study, and life as represented by man as he exists. The questions whence man came and whither he is going never troubled him; he simply looked on man as a member of a society, and strove to work out for himself by the light of ancient records how he might best contribute to his own happiness, and to that of the world in general.

Man, he taught, is master of his own destiny, and not only so, but he is the equal of heaven and earth, and as such is able to influence the course of nature. By complete sincerity he is able to give its full development to his nature. Having done this, he is able to do the same to the nature of other men. Having given its full development to the nature of other men, he can give their full development to the natures of animals and things. Having given their full development to the natures of animals and things, he can assist the transforming and nourishing powers of heaven and earth. Having assisted the transforming and nourishing powers of heaven and earth, he may with heaven and earth form a trinity.[1] Then he becomes the equal of heaven and earth;[2] and when this stage is reached, universal order will prevail, and all things are nourished and perfected.[3]

Such is the position which the ideal man occupies in the universe. And the ideal man is endowed by Heaven with an ideal nature. All men are born good, and all are alike possessed of heaven-sent qualities which enable them to acquire the ideal nature. That which a man inherits is goodness, and when that is perfected, it becomes his nature.[4] As a native commentator remarks, the goodness bestowed by Heaven is like flowing water, which, when a man has perfected himself, is crystallized and becomes his nature. "The great God," said T'ang, "has conferred even on the inferior people a moral sense, by obeying which they attain a constant nature."[5] Or, in other words, Heaven, in giving birth to all people, affixed to everything a corresponding law,[6] which it is the duty of men to watch, listen to, understand and obey. When men do so, ministers and officials will be patriotic, the relations between fathers and sons will be perfected, and the people will maintain a constant nature, by obedience to which their affections will be set on benevolence, righteousness, patriotism, and filial piety. When once the ideal nature is acquired, it is like water of which the fount is perfectly

---

[1] Chung yung, xxii. [2] Chung yung, xxvi. 5.
[3] Chung yung, i. 5. [4] Yih king.
[5] Shoo king, T'ang kaou. [6] She king, Ta ya, Ching min.

clear and without impurities. It undergoes no change, but if it ever should be changed, it cannot be restored to its primitive state. It is the guiding principle of the heart, and finds its development in the affections and desires. And just as the nature of gold is hardness and the nature of fire is heat, so the nature of man is benevolence, righteousness, propriety, wisdom, and faithfulness. There may however be an evil nature, for when King T'ai kea was not able to change his courses, E Yin, his minister, said to himself, "This is unrighteousness and is becoming by practice his nature."[1] This use of the word Sing, Nature, in this passage is however explained away by the commentators, who hold that it means habit, and not nature.

These definitions of man's nature were endorsed by Confucius, who was especially loud in his commendations of that quoted above from the She king. Tsze-kung says, however, that the "master's . . . words about man's nature and the way of heaven cannot be heard;" but this statement is probably due either to the fact that he did not understand what Confucius did say on the subject, or because he was, as the disciples generally were, anxious to eliminate from the teachings of the Master all that they considered to be beyond the intellectual or moral comprehension of the people. Confucius was not a speculative thinker, and therefore we do not find him dwelling to the same length on such speculations as Mencius and some of the late philosophers, but he said quite enough to show that he was in entire harmony on the subject

---

[1] Shoo king, T'sai kea.

with the ancient sages.[1] The natures of all men he taught are nearly alike, that is to say, the conditions of their endowment are not dissimilar, but by practice they get to be wide apart.   He reiterated also the orthodox belief that man's nature is good, and that its inherent goodness is displayed by its affection for the four decorous principles, *i.e.*, humanity, rectitude, propriety, and knowledge. According to him, also, man's nature has an honourable place compared with those of heaven and earth, and is more honourable than that of things. For all things are endowed with distinctive natures, which, however, differ from man's nature in that they are incapable of being cultivated or taught.

The goodness which is inherited from Heaven does not, unfortunately, always remain untainted, but is like running water which knows no stagnation, and is always flowing onward to the sea. Some streams become defiled before they have run far, and others after long courses get defiled, some more some less. But that which cannot be defiled is not water. And so it is with men's natures : they nearly all leave the fountain pure, but become contaminated, some more some less, and some earlier than others, but they are all liable to contamination.

This is true of the great mass of mankind, but there are two classes, the wise of the highest and the stupid of the lowest, who know no change. The gradations from the highest to the lowest class are explained by Confucius to be, " Those who are born

---

[1] Lun yu xvii. 3.

with the possession of knowledge are the highest class of men. Those who learn, and so readily get possession of knowledge, are the next. Those who are dull and stupid, and yet succeed in learning, are another class next to these. While those who are dull and stupid and yet do not learn, are the lowest of the people." [1]

It is among members of the highest class, or Sages, that Nature reaches its highest development. The Sage is born in possession of knowledge and of perfect purity. He obeys without effort the promptings of his nature, and thus maintains a perfect uprightness and pursues the heavenly way without the slightest deflection. He alone, possessing all the sage-like qualities, shows himself quick in apprehension, clear in discernment, of far-reaching intelligence and all-embracing knowledge, fitted to exercise rule ; magnanimous, generous, benign, and mild, fitted to exercise forbearance ; impulsive, energetic, firm and enduring, fitted to maintain a firm hold ; self-adjusted, grave, never swerving from the mean, and correct, fitted to command reverence ; accomplished, distinctive, concentrative, and searching, fitted to exercise discrimination. All-embracing is he and vast, deep and active as a fountain, sending forth in their due seasons his virtues. All-embracing and vast ; he is like heaven. Deep and active as a fountain, he is like the abyss. He is seen, and the people all reverence him ; he speaks, and the people all believe him ; he acts, and the people are all pleased with him. Therefore his

[1] Lun yu, xvi. 9.

fame overspreads the Middle Kingdom, and extends to all barbarous tribes. Wherever ships and carriages reach ; wherever the strength of man penetrates ; wherever the heavens overshadow and the earth sustains ; wherever the sun and moon shine ; wherever frosts and dews fall :—all who have blood and breath unfeignedly honour and love him. Hence it is said : —" He is the equal of Heaven." [1]

This view as held by Confucius is precisely that set forth in the earlier classics, where we are told that just as water flows in moist hollows, and fire approaches dry places ; the clouds follow the dragon, and the winds the tiger, so when the Sage acts, the myriads of things observe him.[2] His virtues equal those of heaven and earth, his brightness is like that of the sun and moon ; his regularity is comparable to that of the four seasons ; and his good and ill-fortune to those of spirits and demons. When he takes the lead of Heaven, Heaven does not rebel, and when he follows Heaven, he observes Heaven's seasons. If Heaven does not rebel against him, much less should men, or spirits, or demons. It is the Sage alone who understands how to advance and to recede, to preserve and to destroy without losing his perfect correctness.[3]

He loves to walk on the heavenly way, and is as steadfast as the way itself ; and just as the sun and moon draw their splendour from heaven and shine everlastingly, so nature catches the reflected wisdom of the Sage and is changed in accordance with his

---

[1] Chung Yung, xxx. 1. [2] Yih king. K'een kwa.
[3] Idem.

likeness.[1] The Sage is thus perfectly virtuous, for he is born without any disposition towards evil, he is adorned with all the accomplishments, and he is infinitely wise.[2] His words are like water, which the more you measure it the deeper it seems, and the more you search for it the further off it appears to be. Again they are like fire, the more you stir it the brighter it becomes, and the more you leave it alone the greater becomes its strength. He gains knowledge without travelling, he describes things without seeing them, and he achieves his purpose without action. His lessons are taught rather by example than by words. He does nothing and the people are straightway transformed ; he has no lusts and the people become spontaneously simple-minded. He delights in practising humility, and because he humbles himself he is exalted, because he avoids display he shines, and because he puts himself last he is first.[3]

It is said, however, that there are circumstances under which Sages may fall from their high estate ; for we are told in the Shoo king that "the Sages of the Shang dynasty by not taking thought became foolish, and the foolish by thinking became sages."[4] The apparent inconsistency in this statement is to be explained by supposing that the process in each case was gradual and extended through many generations. Thus we see that the descendants of the Sage T'ang, who was appointed by Shang-te to be a model to the "nine regions,"[5] gradually fell away until the depth of

---

[1] Yĭh king. Hăng kwo.   [2] Shoo king. Ta yu mow.

[3] Laou-tsze.   [4] Shoo king, To fang.

[5] She king. Shang sung chang fă.

folly and vice was reached in the person of Show, the last of the dynasty; and in the same way we may suppose that Woo Wang's wisdom was the inherited completion of a progressive course of virtue extending over ages.

The qualifications of a Sage being of such surpassing excellence, it is plain that the honour of fellowship with so distinguished a band can be claimed for only a few. Those officially recognized as being holy men or Sages are:—Fuh-he (2852-2737 B.C.); Shin-nung (2737-2697); Hwang-te (2697-2597); Yaou (2356-2255); Shun (2255-2205); Yu (2205-2197); T'ang (1766-1753); Eyin (ab. 1709); Pihe (ab. 1200); Wăn Wang (ab. 1200); Woo Wang (1122-1078); Chow kung (1105); Lew Hea-hwuy (ab. 1600); and Confucius.

All these possessed the spotless and sinless nature which is the gift of Heaven, and which corresponds with man's destiny.

For destiny is that which, together with the principles of benevolence, righteousness, propriety and faith, is bestowed on every man by Heaven. When these principles find their developments in thought and action, they become the ideal nature. After having been metamorphosed by the male and female principles of nature, the destiny is sent forth as life. The completion of the (appointed) transformation and the exhaustion of the (fixed) numbers is death. Therefore destiny is the beginning of nature, and death is the end of life.[1] But life is nature, and therefore destiny is called

---

[1] Kea yu.

the giver and ender of life. In this sense Confucius speaks of his disciple Yen Hwuy. "There was Yen Hwuy; he loved to learn. He did not transfer his anger; he did not repeat a fault. Unfortunately his destiny was short and he died; and now there is not such another."[1] In some instances it appears simply as the equivalent of life, as when Confucius said, "The man who in the view of gain thinks of righteousness; who in the view of danger is prepared to give up his destiny; and who does not forget an old agreement however far back it extends;—such a man may be reckoned a complete man." The gift of destiny to all men launches them in existence with equal advantages, but the cares and temptations of the world affecting them in different ways soon produce variety. It is only a superior man who can arrive at the knowledge of his own destiny; but having done so, he can arrive at the knowledge of the destiny of men and things. For things have destinies as well as men, but, unlike men, they are unable to control their destinies. "If my principles," said Confucius, "are to advance, it is their destiny. If they are to fall to the ground, it is their destiny."[2]

Sometimes destiny is used as meaning only command or appointment. As when we are told that Woo Wang received his destiny to the throne in his old age.[3] But destiny in its true sense is to Heaven what nature is to man. That which Heaven gives is destiny, and that which man receives is nature. Nature, seen in the affairs of life and in things, is right

---

[1] Lun yu, vi. 2.   [2] Lun yu, xiv. 38.
[3] Chung yung, xviii. 3.

principle. Only the man who has exhausted right principles and given full development to nature, can understand the deep and unintermitting destinies of Heaven. It was to this pitch that Confucius says he arrived when he was fifty years of age.

The same Heaven who is the bestower of destiny is also the creator of all things. By its power all creation grows and flourishes, and under its influence human beings and things arrive at perfection. It is the subtle, ethereal fire which dwells in the highest heaven,[1] and yet humbles itself to behold the things which are upon earth. With perfect impartiality and infinite spiritual wisdom it watches over the happiness and the sufferings of the people, and the excellences and wrongs of kings and governors. Nothing passes unheard or unseen by it, though it neither hearkens nor looks. No darkness conceals from its view, and no privacy hides from its knowledge.[2] By Heaven the virtuous are rewarded and the guilty are punished. Kings rule by its sufferance, and are deposed by its decree. "Moved with indignation at the crime of King Show, Great Heaven," we are told in the Shoo-king, "charged King Wăn to display its majesty, and to destroy the tyrant." Out of love for the people Heaven appoints rulers to protect and instruct them, that they may assist Shang-te in securing the tranquillity of the four quarters of the world. Heaven is unpitying, as when it sent down ruin on Yin, and brought to nought the dynasty of Hea.[3] Its favour

---

[1] Yih king. K'een kwa.   [2] Shoo king. Shoo ming.
[3] Shoo king.

is not easily preserved, neither is it to be trusted. Only by carefully following the heavenly way can its smiles be propitiated, and only by a sedulous performance of the five duties, and the ceremonies attaching to the social distinctions, which it has itself ordained, can its goodwill be secured. For those, however, who thus obey the dictates of their destiny and develop the ideal human nature, which is the heritage of all, Heaven has in store long life and riches and honour.

But man is in one sense independent of Heaven, and the Sage is, as we have seen, the equal of Heaven. It has laid down certain laws which, if any man obey, he may claim as a right all the blessings which Heaven has to give. Prayer is unnecessary, because Heaven does not actively interfere with the soul of man. It has endowed him at his birth with goodness, which may, if he will, become his nature, and his true destiny may thus be realized. But all this is to be accomplished by his own efforts. In common with all created things, he forms part of Heaven, and by fulfilling his destiny he is able to assist the transforming and nourishing powers of Heaven and earth.[1] Even the length of his days is in his own hands, for it is not Heaven that cuts man's life short, but by the results of his own conduct it is brought to an end.

Some few passages in the Confucian Analects and elsewhere seem to invest Heaven with more of the character of a personal god; as, for example, when the warden at E said to the disciples, "Heaven is

---

[1] Chung yung, xxii.

going to use your master as an alarm-bell;" or again when Confucius said, "While Heaven does not let the cause of truth perish, what can the people of K'wang do to me?" But the preponderating evidence goes to show that Heaven is but the equivalent of Providence, which orders but does not direct.

Dividing with Heaven the worship of men, and holding an intermediate position between the two, stand spirits and demons. History does not reach back to a time when these spirits of the air were not worshipped. Fuh-he, we are told, sacrificed to them, and the "Book of History" contains numberless references to them. The *She-ke*, or Historical Record, says that in the beginning the spirits were the associates of men, and when Chow-kung intercedes for the life of his brother King Woo, he addresses himself to the spirits of his father, grandfather, and great-grandfather, and advances as a reason why his life should be taken rather than that of the king, that he possesses the qualities which fit him more especially to wait on the spirits. This deification of deceased men was accepted as a common belief. Confucius, we are told, sacrificed to the dead as though they were present, and to the spirits as though they were before him. [1] But to sacrifice to the spirit of a stranger he looked upon as flattery. [2] The spirits, then, are interested only in those things which concern the welfare of their descendants on earth, and thus, while in the case of private individuals the spirits watch over their family affairs, the souls of

[1] Lun yu, iii. 12.   [2] Lun yu, ii. 24.

departed emperors are consulted in all matters relating to the duties of government devolving on their imperial representative. In the Shoo king we are told that the Emperor Shun, in announcing an important decision, said, "I consulted and deliberated with all my ministers and people. The spirits signified their assent, the tortoise and the grass (instruments of divination) having both concurred."

All national events of importance are to this day announced by the emperor to the spirits. Dr. Legge, in his paper on "Confucianism in Relation to Christianity," quotes a prayer addressed to the spirits by an emperor of the Ming dynasty (1538 A.D.), when about to make a slight change in the title by which Shang-te was addressed : "Beforehand we inform you, all ye celestial and all ye terrestrial spirits," he prayed, "and will trouble you on our behalf, to exert your spiritual influences, and display your vigorous efficacy communicating our poor desire to Shang-te, and praying him mercifully to grant us his acceptance and regard, and to be pleased with the title which we shall reverently present."

This prayer was addressed not only to the ancestral spirits, but to those of heaven and earth, of hills and rivers, and of land and grain, all of which require that offerings should be made to them. But they by no means accept sacrifice indiscriminately. Entire sincerity is required of them who approach the altar, and only the sacrifices of those who fulfil this condition are accepted by them.[1] "Of old," we are told

---

· Shoo king.

in the Shoo king, " the earlier sovereign of the Hea dynasty cultivated earnestly their virtue, and then there were no calamities from Heaven. The spirits of the hills and rivers were likewise all in tranquillity." To arrive at this state of harmony with the spirits should be the object of every one, for it is only by so doing that the good-will of Heaven can be obtained. "The King of Hea," says the Shoo king, "could not maintain the virtue of his predecessors unchanged, but contemned the spirits and oppressed the people. Wherefore Heaven no longer extended its protection to him ; but looked out among the myriad regions to give its guidance to one who might receive its favour, fondly seeking a possessor of pure virtue, whom it might make lord over all the spirits."

On the subject of spirits, as on all matters relating to heavenly beings, Confucius was reticent. His mind was wrapt up in the things of this earth, and he looked upon all such subjects as obscure and unprofitable. That they were worthy of reverence he was ready to affirm, but he considered that constant reference to them was likely to lead to superstition. "Spirits are to be respected," he said, "but to be kept at a distance ;" and in reply to a question put to him as to serving the spirits, he answered, "While you are not able to serve men, how can you serve their spirits ? " But though he was opposed to superstitious meddling with spirits, he was yet fully conscious of their constant presence. "How abundant," he said, "is the capacity of spiritual beings. We look for them, but do not see them; we listen for them, but do not hear them : yet they enter

G

into all things, and there is nothing without them. They cause the people of the empire to fast and purify themselves, and to array themselves in their richest dresses in order to attend at their sacrifices. Then, like overflowing water, they seem to be over the heads and on the right and left of their worshippers."

The worship of spirits, however, takes the shape rather of respectful recognition of their existence than of devotional address to a godhead. They have no power of themselves to influence the fates of men, and even in some cases men are placed as lords over them, but reverence or want of reverence to them is rewarded or punished by Heaven. Sometimes, however, as in the prayer quoted above, they act as intercessors between man and Shang-te, and in this way occupy a parallel position to the saints of the Roman calendar.

But the highest object of worship among the ancient Chinese was Shang-te, who approached nearer to the idea of the Hebrew God than any of their divinities. Heaven was high and great, but Shang-te ruled both heaven and earth. It was by his favour that sovereigns ruled and nations prospered, and it was at his decree that thrones were upset and kingdoms were brought to nought. As an earthly sovereign rules over a kingdom, so Shang-te lords it over the azure heaven![1]

The worship of Shang-te is the most ancient, as well as the most sacred form of Chinese worship. During the reign of Hwang-te (2697 B.C.) a temple

---

[1] Kin koo t'oo shoo tseih ch'ing.   Shin e teen.

was erected to his honour, and a century later music was added to the rites performed at his altar. When the sovereign worshipped before him, he wore a fur dress and a crown, and offered up on a round hillock a first-born male as a whole burnt sacrifice.[1] It was to him that prayer was made in all great emergencies, and in the eyes of the Emperor and people he appeared as a personal God, directing their ways, supporting them in their difficulties, and chastising them for their faults. When T'ang the founder of the Shang dynasty (1766 B.C.), overthrew the iniquitous Kё̆, the last ruler of the Hea dynasty, he defended himself from the charge of rebellion by making a proclamation, in which he said, " The sovereign of Hea was an offender, and as I fear Shang-te I dare not but punish him." Again speaking to his people he said, " The good in you I will not dare to conceal, and for the evil in me I will not dare to forgive myself; I will examine these things in harmony with the mind of Shang-te."[2] T'ang's belief in the personal interference of Shang-te in the affairs of man is plainly stated when he says, " The ways of Shang-te are not invariable; he showers down blessings on the good, and pours down miseries on the evil."[3]

But as time went on the distinctive belief in the personality of Shang-te became obscured, and he was degraded from his supremacy to the level of the impersonal heaven. In fact, later commentators affirm that Shang-te is Heaven, Azure Heaven, the Greatest Deity in the Purple Obscure Palace, the most honoured

---

[1] Chow le. [2] Shoo king. [3] Ditto.

one of Heaven,—all of which titles give but a very imperfect idea of the position he held in the sight of Yaou and of Shun and of the ancient Sages.

Unfortunately on this point also Confucius departed from the higher faith of his ancestors, and by sanctioning the worship of spirits, and omitting all mention of Shang-te, he reduced that deity to his position of one among the host of heaven. Once only does he speak of Shang-te, and then it was only to state the fact that "by the ceremonies of the sacrifices to heaven and earth the kings Wăn and Woo served Shang-te, and by the ceremonies of the ancestral temple they sacrificed to their ancestors." This remark shows that Confucius perceived that the various religious rites practised by the ancients had for their object the worship of the one God, but he allowed this knowledge to remain sterile. He deduced nothing from it either to spiritualize his teachings or to elevate his practice. The example of the earthly course run by the ancient Sages was sufficient in his own case to lead him into the same paths of virtue, and he committed the mistake of supposing that the same cause would produce a like effect in all men.

Starting with the belief that all men are born equally good, there is, more excuse for the adopting of such a doctrine by Confucius than can be advanced for many later philosophers who have practically held the same view. But even he admitted that the temptations of the world and the flesh were apt to sully the original purity of man, and his experiences at the different courts he visited should have taught him that headlong passions, vicious habits, and weak wills, need some stronger corrective than the contemplation of the virtue of Yaou and the purity of Shun.

In spite, however, of the silence of Confucius on the subject of Shang-te, his worship has been maintained, not perhaps in its original purity, but with marks of reverence which place its object on the highest pinacle of the Chinese Pantheon. At the present day the Imperial worship of Shang-te on the round hillock to the south of the city of Peking is surrounded with all the solemnity of which such an occasion is capable. "The altar is a beautiful marble structure, ascended by 27 steps, and ornamented by circular balustrades on each of its three terraces. On it is raised a magnificent triple-roofed circular structure, 99 feet in height, which constitutes the most conspicuous object in the *tout ensemble*. . . These structures are deeply enshrined in a thick cypress grove—reminding the visitor of the custom which formerly prevailed among the heathen nations of the Old Testament, and of the solemn shade which surrounded some celebrated temples of ancient Greece. On the day before the sacrifices the Emperor proceeds to the Hall of Fasting, on the west side of the south altar. Here he spends the night in watching and meditation, after first inspecting the offerings. The tablets to the Supreme Ruler of Heaven (*i.e.* Shang-te), and to the Emperor's ancestors, are preserved in the chapel at the back of each altar. There are no images. Both these chapels are circular, and tiled with blue glazed porcelain . . . The south altar the most important of all Chinese religious structures, has the following dimensions. It consists of a triple circular terrace, 210 ft. wide at the base, 150 in the middle, and 90 at the top. In these notice the multiples of three: $3 \times 3 = 9$, $3 \times 5 = 15$, $3 \times 7 = 21$. The heights of the three terraces, upper, middle, and lower, are 5·72 feet, 6·23 feet, and 5 feet respectively. At the time of sacrificing, the tablets to Heaven and to the Emperor's ancestors are placed on the top; they are 2 feet 5 inches long and 5 inches wide. The title is in gilt letters; that of Heaven faces the south, and those of the ancestors east and west. The Emperor, with his immediate suite, kneels in front of the tablet to Shang-te, and faces the north. The platform is laid with marble stones, forming nine concentric circles; the inner circle consists of nine stones, cut so as to fit with close edges round the central stone, which is a perfect circle. Here the Emperor kneels, and is surrounded first by the circles of the terraces and their enclosing walls, and then by the circle of the horizon. He thus seems to himself and his court to be in the centre of the universe, and, turning to the north, assuming the attitude of a subject, he acknowledges in prayer and by his position that he is inferior to Heaven, and to Heaven alone. Round him on the pavement are the nine circles of as many heavens, consisting of nine stones, then eighteen, then twenty-seven, and so on in successive multiples of nine till the square of nine, the favourite number of Chinese philosophy, is reached in the outermost circle of eighty-one stones. . . . As might be expected, careful distinctions are made in the sacrifices. The animals ordinarily used for food by the ancient

Chinese, and the fruits of the earth known to them, are almost all included. But productions recently introduced into the country are not offered. To Heaven alone is offered a piece of blue jade, cylindrical in shape and a foot long, formerly used as a symbol of sovereignty. But the great distinguishing sign of superiority is the offering of a whole burnt sacrifice to Heaven."[1]

Next to the Sage in the scale of Confucian humanity is the superior man, but unlike the Sage his distinctive characteristics were unrecognized until pointed out by Confucius. From the dawn of history we hear of Sages, but such a being as the superior man, as portrayed in the Four Books, finds no place in the Shoo king. Twice only does the expression occur as pointing to a separate order. Once we are told that " When a prince treats superior men with familiarity, he cannot get them to give him all their hearts."[2] And again, "The superior man will have no luxurious ease."[3] But it was left to Confucius to develop the superior man who forms a leading feature in the Confucian philosophy. The Sage was incapable of evil. Born with a perfectly pure nature, he had but to follow the dictates of his will to walk in the paths of virtue. No temptations to evil assailed him, and no allurements led him aside. But the superior man was not so; he was subject to faults and failings which, though they were as transient as the eclipses of the sun and moon

---

[1] Peking, by the Rev. J. Edkins.   [2] Shoo-king, Leu-gaou.
[3] Shoo-king.   Woo-yih.

were yet equally observable by all men.[1]   He was endowed with no special grace by nature, but by carefully perfecting the good originally implanted in him, his "way became identical with that of Heaven and earth and of all things,"[2] and he arrived at the dignity of a superior man.

Nine things he strove after: in seeing to see clearly, in hearing to hear distinctly, in expression to be benign, in his demeanour to be decorous, in speaking to be sincere, in his duties to be respectful, in doubt to inquire, in resentment to think of difficulties, when he saw an opportunity for gain to think of righteousness.[3]   Three things he avoided: in youth, when the physical powers are not settled, he avoided lust; in manhood, when the physical powers are in full vigour, he avoided quarrelsomeness ; in old age, when the animal powers are decayed, he avoided covetousness.[4]

The superior man was righteous in all his ways; his acts were guided by the laws of propriety, and were marked by strict sincerity.[5]   Being without reproach, he was also without fear, and having studied deeply, his mind was untroubled by doubt or misgiving.   Nothing put him out of countenance, for wisdom, humanity, and valour were his constant companions.   Of the ordinances of Heaven, of great men, and of the words of Sages, he alone stood in respectful awe, and this not out of servility, but because he possessed sufficient knowledge to com-

---

[1] Lun yu, xix. 20.   [2] Chung yung, xii. 4.
[3] Lun yu, xvi. 10.   [4] Ibid. xvi. 7.
[5] Ibid. xv. 17.

prehend the wisdom embodied in those powers. Mere eloquence had no effect upon him, and he was careless about the animal comforts of this life. He laughed at want, for his aims were directed towards "the heavenly way," not towards eating; and for the same reason wealth and poverty were not causes of anxiety to him. He loved to associate with those among his equals who were students and scholars, and sought to perfect his virtue by converse with his friends. He never hesitated to improve his knowledge by inquiry; he studied the past and was acquainted with the present. He was exacting only of himself, and was distressed by his want of ability. The neglect of his contemporaries did not affect him, but the thought that he had so failed in virtue as not to leave a name behind him troubled him greatly.

Confucius even admitted that he had failed to reach the level of the superior man. "In the way of the superior man," he said, "there are four things to not one of which have I as yet attained:—To serve my father as I would require my son to serve me; to serve my elder brother as I would require my younger brother to serve me; to behave to a friend as I would require him to behave to me. Earnest in practising the ordinary virtues, and careful in speaking about them; if, in his conduct, he has anything defective, the superior man dares not but exert himself; and if, in his words, he has any excess, he dares not allow himself such license. Thus his words have respect to his actions, and his actions have respect to his words; is it not complete sincerity which makes the superior man?"[1]

The superior man is constantly striving to improve himself, and thus Confucius compared him to a traveller who has to traverse every step of the way which leads him to his destination, or to a mountaineer, who, in order to reach the top of the peak, has to start from the foot. In this way he made sure and steady progress, and was calm and quiet, patiently waiting for the appointments of Heaven. Mean men, on the contrary, love to walk in dangerous paths, and prefer to look for the occurrence of some lucky event rather than enjoy that happy confidence which is the portion of those who walk in the "heavenly way." If, however, at any time the feet of the superior man should slip, he acts like "the archer who, when he misses the centre of the target, turns round and seeks for the cause of failure in himself."

When asked what constituted the superior man, Confucius said : "He cultivates himself so as to give rest to the people." The welfare of the people was the constant care of Confucius and his followers, and the main object of their philosophy was so to order themselves as by the force of their example to turn men from their evil ways and thoughts to the pursuit of virtue. Then we are told that a superior man was humble in his conduct, respectful to his superiors, kind in nourishing the people, and just in ordering them. He rarely quarrelled, but when he did, he

[1] Chung yung, xiii.

maintained his character, and his hatred was directed only against those whose conduct made them worthy objects of disdain. He hated those who proclaim the evils of others. He hated those who, being in a low station, slander their superiors. He hated those who possess valour unbalanced by the observance of propriety. And he hated those who are forward and determined, and, at the same time, of contracted understanding.

Such were some of the leading characteristics of the superior man, and, according to the teachings of Confucius, he occupied no unattainable level. The way to arrive at the position of a superior man was open to all, and the steps to be trodden were clearly marked out. What those steps were we will proceed to describe in the following chapter.

CHAPTER IV.

THE TRAINING NECESSARY TO BECOME A "SUPERIOR MAN."

THE various stages of moral advancement which it is necessary to go through before the level of the superior man can be reached are thus laid down in " The Great Learning :"—" The ancients . . . wishing to be sincere in their thoughts, first extended to the utmost their knowledge. Such extension of knowledge lay in the investigation of things. Things being investigated, knowledge became complete. Their knowledge being complete, their thoughts were sincere. Their thoughts being sincere, their hearts were then rectified. Their hearts being rectified, their persons were cultivated. Their persons being cultivated, their families were regulated. Their families being regulated, their states were rightly governed. Their states being rightly governed, the whole empire was made tranquil and happy."

To effect the tranquillity and happiness of the empire was the main object of the teaching of Confucius, and as this result can only be obtained through the agency of superior men, except on the rare occasions when sages appear on the stage, it follows that they form the centre figures in his philosophy. Their progress is from the near to the far, and each step must be made sure of before any further advance may be attempted. A prince, says the Le ke, who wishes to transform his people must begin by learning. This is the foundation upon which the future edifice must be built. There are no royal roads to the acquisition of the "heavenly way." If a man has sumptuous viands laid before him and does not eat them, he does not know their lusciousness; and if a man were to arrive at the "heavenly way" without learning, he would not understand its excellence.[1] But a man can no more arrive at the "heavenly way" without learning, than a gem can be turned to some use without being cut.[2]

No pursuit can be acquired, and no virtue can remain untainted, without learning. If a man does not learn to play in tune, he cannot harmonize the chords; if he does not study metaphor, he cannot write poetry; if he does not study the various colours of clothes, he cannot conform to the rules of propriety; if the arts are not flourishing, he cannot take pleasure in learning. Therefore a superior man treasures up learning, he improves, rests, and is satisfied;[3] for to be fond of learning is to be near to knowledge.[4] Without it benevolence becomes folly, wisdom vagueness, sincerity recklessness, straightforwardness rudeness, boldness disorder, and firmness foolishness.[5]

But study must be pursued with discretion, and

---

[1] Le ke.   [2] Ibid.   [3] Ibid.
[4] Chung yung, xx. 10.   [5] Lun yu, xvii. 8, 3

can no more be divorced from thought than thought can be from it. "Learning without thought," said Confucius, "is labour lost; thought without learning is perilous."[1] The exercise of independent thought formed no part in the Confucian system. Complete wisdom was to be found only among the ancient sages, and it followed therefore that the truest means of acquiring the highest knowledge was by contemplating the deeds and sayings of those worthies. By no mental endeavour could any man hope to surpass or even to equal the supreme wisdom of Yaou and of Shun, and his surest way of acquiring a trace of the divine afflatus must be by studying and meditating on their careers. "I have been the whole day," said Confucius, "without eating, and the whole night without sleeping, occupied with thinking. But it was of no use. The better plan is to learn."[2]

The supreme object of learning should be truth, and incidentally self-improvement and the knowledge of one's own faults. These are best to be acquired, according to Confucius, by studying the conduct of the holy and just men of antiquity, "The Book of Odes," "The Rules of Propriety," and the "Book of Changes." Of this last he said, as quoted above: "If some years were added to my life, I would give fifty to the study of the Book of Changes, and then I might come to be without great faults." By study therefore a man should learn to recognize his faults and to expose the inequalities in his disposition, and then to clear the ground for an advance towards virtue.

[1] Lun yu, ii. 15.   [2] Ibid. xv. 30.

By the pursuit of learning knowledge may be completed, and thus a perfect understanding of the principles of things may be obtained. Such knowledge must be thorough, and must be arrived at by research. It should embrace all subjects, from the highest to the lowest. Confucius said that at the age of fifty he knew the destinies of heaven. Heaven itself is also to be known; and to know men was one of the Sage's definitions of knowledge, the want of which is a far greater cause for regret than being unknown by men. But a man should be quite certain what he knows and what he does not know. "Yew, shall I teach you what knowledge is?" said Confucius. "When you know a thing, to hold that you know it; and when you do not know a thing, to allow that you do not know it;—this is knowledge." Thus, as Chwang-tsze put it, a man ought to stand firm like a chair on four legs, all of which are strong and of even length; but a man who is uncertain or imperfect in his knowledge, is like a chair which, having lost a leg, or which stands unevenly on its feet, is useless as a support.

The study of history is a fruitful source of knowledge. Confucius, according to Tze-kung, acquired his knowledge by the contemplation of the doctrines and conduct of kings Wăn and Woo. The regulations of the Hea dynasty may be known, said Confucius, by studying those of the Yin dynasty. The regulations of the Yin may be known by studying those of the Chow, and the regulations of the Chow may be known by studying those of dynasties which follow after, even at the distance of a hundred ages.

But something more must be arrived at besides mere knowledge. "A man's knowledge," said Confucius, "may be sufficient to attain, but if he has not virtue enough to enable him to hold, he will lose whatever he may have gained. And even if his virtue should be sufficient to enable him to hold, if he should be unable to govern with dignity, the people will not respect him. Again, if his knowledge and virtue should be sufficient, and he should be able to govern with dignity, yet if he try to move the people contrary to the rules of propriety, full excellence is not reached." But true knowledge should enable a man to distinguish between truth and falsehood, and to assimilate all that is good, and to discard all that is evil, in that which he learns. More than this, however, is required by him : he must love the truth as well as know it, and must delight in it as well as love it. Then he may be said to have completed himself, and all created things. This is the completion of knowledge.

By the completion of this true knowledge the thoughts and intentions of the heart become sincere. By this is meant, as we are told in "The Great Learning" (vi. 1), "allowing no self-deception, as when we hate a bad smell, and as we love what is beautiful. This is called enjoyment in oneself. Therefore the superior man must be watchful over himself when he is-alone." The thoughts or intentions are such as proceed out of the heart, and he who wishes to rectify his heart must first make his intentions sincere, just as a man whose house is entered by burglars first turns out the thieves, and then looks after the welfare of his family; or as a farmer first weeds his land before putting in his seed.[1]

The character " E," meaning thought or intention, differs little in meaning, the commentators tell us, from " Tsing," desires, and " Che," the will. " E " is rather the incipient form of " Che." The man who wishes to be pleased or to be angry exercises his " E," but the man who *is* pleased or angry exercises his " Che."[2] " Che " is, therefore, the positive form of " E," and it is all-important that it should be sincere. If a man's intentions are not settled, he is like a ship without a compass, or a horse without a bridle. But the intentions of man are as often fixed on what is evil as on what is good, and therefore they should strive to arrive at the same intentions as those of E Yin, whose delight was in the Taou of Yaou and Shun,[3] or as the Shoo-king (Leu yaou) puts it, " the intentions should repose in what is right, and words should be listened to according to their relation to right." The wishes and intentions of the heart must be directed only towards that which is right; and if the will be set on virtue, there will be no practice of wickedness.[4] Nothing can lead astray a man whose will is fixed. " The commander of a large state," said Confucius, " may be carried off, but the will of even a common man cannot be taken from him."[5] He may, however, yield to temptation and surrender his will, as, according to Confucius, did " Hwuy and Shaou-leen,

---

[1] Kin koo t'oo shoo tseih ch'ing. Heŏ hing teen.
[2] Ibid. [3] Ibid.
[4] Lun yu, iv. 4. [5] Ibid. ix. 25.

H

who surrendered their will and submitted to taint in their persons, but yet their words corresponded with reason, and their actions are such as men are anxious to see."[1] But the surest foundation on which to establish the will is learning. "At fifteen," said Confucius, "my mind was bent on learning. At thirty I stood firm. At forty I had no doubts. At fifty I knew the decrees of Heaven. At sixty my ear was an obedient organ for the reception of truth. And at seventy I could follow what my heart desired without transgressing what was right."[2]

The combination of extensive learning and a will firmly and sincerely set on the paths of duty, will surely lead a man forward in the course of virtue. Having completed his knowledge, he is able to arrive at a distinct appreciation of truth; and having bent his mind earnestly on the pursuit of truth, he is on the high way to rectify his heart.

Though not taking so pronounced a view of the wickedness of the heart of man as the Psalmist, Confucianists hold that "it is restless and prone to err, and that its affinity for the right way is small."[3] For out of it proceed pleasure, anger, sorrow, and joy,[4] all of which, when not kept under proper control, are apt to disturb the harmony which should reign in the mind of the superior man. These evil passions have been likened by Choo He to the mud which lies at the bottom of a tub, leaving the water on the surface clear and bright; but when temptations

---

[1] Lun yu, xviii. 8.
[2] Ibid. ii. 4.
[3] Shoo-king, Ta Yu mow.
[4] Chung yung, 1. 4.

arise which stir them, up then the whole body of water becomes turbid and impure. Thus we are told in the Shoo-king that the officers of Yin, in the confidence of their prideful extravagance, extinguished their sense of righteousness and displayed before men the beauty of their robes, proud, licentious, arrogant and boastful: the natural result was that they should end in being thoroughly bad. And though their lost hearts have been in a measure recovered it is difficult to keep them under proper restraint.[1] Or, as it is said in "The Great Learning," if a man be under the influence of passion he will be incorrect in his conduct. He will be the same if he is under the influence of terror, or under the influence of fond regard, or under that of sorrow and distress. When the mind (heart) is not present, we look and do not see, we hear and do not understand, we eat and do not know the taste of what we eat.[2]

The remedy against these disturbing causes is to follow out the true line of conduct,[3] as pointed out by knowledge, and the way to which should have been previously cleared by making sincere the thoughts and intentions of the heart. But, above all things, virtue must be true virtue, for then only will the heart be at ease. The least admixture of hypocrisy will but add trouble to trouble, and stupidity to stupidity.[4] But the man who orders his affairs with righteousness, and his heart with propriety, will not only be advantaged in this life, but

[1] Shoo-king, Peih ming.   [2] Ta heŏ, vii. 12.
[3] Shoo-king, Pwan kang.   [4] Shoo-king, Chow kwan.

will transmit a grand example to posterity.[1] That temporal blessings flow from the exercise of virtue is an article of faith which is found everywhere in the old Confucian works. The Book of Odes points at the outward propriety of king Wăn as the natural result of his maintaining in his heart a profound devotion to his duties,[2] and the blessings which accompanied his reign to his having watchfully and reverently served God with complete intelligence.[3] In his case, as in the case of every superior man, "riches adorned his house and virtue his person. His heart was expanded and his body was at ease."[4]

But the issues of the heart find their expression in the affections and desires, and it is therefore necessary that these should be set on what is right. A man who is ripening for a superior man will then love learning, for out of it come the springs of knowledge. But, above all things, his heart will be set on virtue, for with this there is nothing which can be compared.[5] He will love also righteousness, propriety, and good faith. And if these ends be pursued in perfect sincerity, and with a mind free from the alloy of self-deception or hypocrisy, it may be said that the heart of such a one is rectified.

The next step in the gradual advance towards perfection is the cultivation of the person. This is a grand turning point in the Confucian "way," and from it a new departure is taken. Up to this stage

---

[1] Shoo-king, Chung hwuy che kaou.
[2] She king, Odes of Yung.   [3] She king, Ta ya.
[4] Ta heŏ, vi. 4.   [5] Lun yu, iv. 6, 1.

the individual has been busy only with his own improvement; but the cultivation of the person influences primarily those around him, and ultimately the whole empire. Every one, therefore, should carefully cultivate his person, having a due regard for others besides himself,[1] and more especially is this the case with a sovereign, who, by cultivating his person with sincere virtue, brings all his subjects into harmonious concord with himself.[2] The cultivation of the person must begin with introspection. Each man must carefully guard his words and watch his conduct. He must fly all that is base and disquieting, and must take benevolence as his dwelling-place, righteousness as his road, propriety as his garment, wisdom as his lamp, and faithfulness as his charm.[3] Confucius said that dignity, reverence, loyalty, and faithfulness made up the qualities of a cultivated man. His dignity separates him from the crowd : being reverent, he is beloved ; being loyal, he is submitted to ; and being faithful, he is trusted.

But all these qualities naturally find expression in words and conduct, and it is to the perfecting of these, therefore, that men must primarily give their attention. They must be earnest in what they are doing, and careful in their speech ;[4] and, above all, things, their conduct must agree with their words ; for if their conduct excels their words, wisdom will not be found in their utterances ; and if their words excel their conduct, they will commit an irreparable

[1] Shoo-king, Kaou-yaou mow.   [2] Shoo-king, T'ae kea.
[3] Lew Heang, Shwŏ yuen.   [4] Lun yu, i. 14.

injury on righteousness.[1] Words and conduct, though the outcome of the individual, spread in their effects far and wide among the people. They are the sources of influence to the superior man, and when manifested, rule over glory and shame.[2] By his words, said Confucius, the superior man directs men, and by his conduct he warns them.

But in order that he may do this, his words must be sincere[3] and carefully weighed. He must be cautious and slow in his speech,[4] which must always be to the point, and such as is appropriate to the occasion. "Confucius," we are told, "in his village, looked simple and sincere, and as if he were one who was not able to speak. When he was in the prince's ancestral temple, or in the court, he spoke minutely on every point, but cautiously. When he was waiting at court, in speaking with the officers of the lower grade, he spoke freely, but in a straightforward manner; in speaking with the officers of the higher grade, he did so blandly, but precisely."[5]

Quoting from the Shoo-king, Confucius said: "Fine words and an insinuating appearance are seldom associated with true virtue."[6] Where virtue is, there will be corresponding words; but it by no means follows that virtue is the invariable con comitant of plausible speech. Confucius began life, he tells us, by judging of men's character by their words, but afterwards he weighed their words by the

---

[1] Lew Heang, Shwŏ yuen.
[2] Yih-king, He tsze.
[3] Lun yu, i. 14.
    Ibid. xii. 3, 2.
[5] Ibid. x. 1.
[6] Ibid. i. 3.

light of their conduct.[1] But words are not to be despised, for it is by them that we learn to know men, and the utterances of the superior man are examples for all ages.

It is a shame to a superior man when his conduct is not in accord with his words.[2] Complete sincerity and scrupulous care should characterize both. He should be forbearing, gentle, and forgiving.[3] "Is there one word," asked Tsze-kung, "which may serve as a rule of practice for all one's life? The master said, Is not reciprocity such a word? What you do not want done to yourself, do not do to others."[4] But, practically, Confucius converted this negative into a positive form when he said: "In the way of the superior man there are four things, to none of which have I as yet attained—To serve my father as I would require my son to serve me; to serve my prince as I would require my minister to serve me; to serve my elder brother as I would require my younger brother to serve me; and to offer first to friends what one requires of them."[5]

If the conduct of a man is sincere, it will be but the outward and visible sign of the virtue which is in him. Above all things, it is necessary that a man should possess virtue. It must be cultivated, cherished, improved, and firmly grasped, for without it the highest careers must fail, and the proudest ruler must be brought low.[6] It is powerful enough

---

[1] Lun yu, v. 9, 2.
[2] Le ke.
[3] Chung yung, x. 3.
[4] Lun yu, xv. 23.
[5] Chung yung, xiii. 4.
[6] Lun yu, xiii, 22.

to move heaven, and there is no distance to which it does not reach.[1] The report of Shun's mysterious virtue, says the Shoo-king, was heard on high, and he was appointed to occupy the imperial seat. But virtue is even more powerful than this, for it places its possessor on a level with the deity, as T'ang, through being always zealous in the reverent cultivation of his virtue, was the fellow of God.[2]

Firmly convinced that the virtue of a sovereign, like that of Kaou-Yaou, descends upon the people as rain or dew upon the earth, fertilizing the soil of their hearts by his gracious example, Confucianists hold that the government of a country is a test of the virtue of the king.[3] Let but his virtue be daily renewed, and not only the people of the empire but the subjects of all the neighbouring states will love him; but, on the other hand, should he be full of his own will, he will be abandoned by even the nine classes of his kindred.[4] Thus the prince who rules by means of it is like the north polar star, which keeps its place, and all the stars turn towards it.[5] The wild tribes on all sides willingly acknowledge their subjection to him,[6] and his throne will be established in wisdom, for he who practises virtue is not left to stand alone,[7] but has always at his command the services of the wisest men in the empire.[8]

---

[1] Shoo-king, Ta Yu mow.   [2] Shoo-king, T'ae kea.

[3] Shoo-king, Ta Yu mow.   [4] Shoo-king, Yu kung.

[5] Lun yu, ii. I.   [6] Shoo-king, Leu gaou.

[7] Lun yu, 4.   Shoo-king, Kaou yaou mow.

Virtue is the first principle of man's nature, and joy is the effulgence of virtue, says the Le ke. But virtue conforms to no invariable model, and is necessarily limited by the capabilities for good possessed by each individual.[1] Confucius described it as consisting of knowledge, humanity, and valour ;[2] and on another occasion he said, "Hold faithfulness and sincerity as first principles, and follow after righteousness ; this is the way to exalt virtue."[3] But fortunately for all who desire to seek it, though it is very lofty, it is also very humble. Confucius himself declared that he dare not rank himself with the Sage and the man of complete virtue, but the standard which he set before himself was "the highest point of virtuous action," such as actuated T'ae-pih, the eldest son of King T'ae, who "thrice declined the empire, and the people in ignorance of his motives could not express their approbation of his conduct."[4] On the other hand, it may be described as doing one's duty. In the time in which Confucius lived virtue was at a low ebb. The practice of it was rare, and love for it was well-nigh extinct,[5] except among those "weak brethren," "the good careful people of the villages, who are the thieves of virtue."[6]

But to any one who is really in earnest in his pursuit of virtue it is not far to seek, and when it is found it is a treasure of great price. It is better than

[1] Shoo-king, Heen yew yĭh tih.
[2] Chung yung, xx. 8.   [3] Lun yu, xii. 10, 1.
[4] Ibid. viii. 1.   [5] Ibid. xv. 12 ; xvii. 13.
[6] Ibid. xv. 8.

life, and riches and honour are not to be compared with it. It gives rest to the heart, and places its possessor above the cares of this life, with its appetites and lusts. It is silent in its operation, and needs no herald to announce its presence. "The doings of supreme heaven have neither sound nor smell. This is perfect virtue."[1] The prominence given by Confucius to valour as a component part of virtue is evidence of the position he holds rather as a politician than as a moral philosopher. His leading idea was the preservation of the State. To this all his teachings tend, and those qualities therefore which might be expected to lead to this end are naturally estimated by him at a high value. Not that his idea of valour was confined only to mere physical courage. On the contrary, he laid great stress on the moral courage which enables a man to throw aside his faults and failings, and to declare plainly in the face of temptations and ridicule that he is seeking after righteousness. "To go on the water and face dragons," said he, "is the valour of the fisherman; to hunt on land, and not avoid rhinoceroses and tigers, is the valour of the huntsman; to face encounters with deadly weapons, and to regard death as life, is the valour of the soldier; but to recognize that poverty comes by the ordinance of Heaven, and that there is a tide in the affairs of men, and in the face of difficulty not to fear, is the valour of the sage."[2]

The highest kind of valour is that, therefore, which

---

[1] Chung yung, xxxiii. 6.　　　　　Kung-tsze, Kea yu.

is accompanied by knowledge; and this kind was conspicuously displayed by Confucius when he and his followers were attacked by overwhelming numbers at Kwang. In reply to the expressions of alarm for his safety uttered by his followers, he said, "After the death of King Wăn, was not the cause of truth lodged in me? If Heaven had wished to let this cause perish, then I should not have been placed in this relation to it. While Heaven does not let the cause of truth perish, what can the people of Kwang do to me?"

When the country is at peace, says the Le ke, valour is utilized in establishing propriety and righteousness, and when the country is disturbed it is employed in fighting and overcoming. Thus valour may and should be used at all times, for if not employed it induces men to be unruly and rebellious.[1] For valour which is not kept in bounds by reason ends in disorder and licentiousness;[2] men's hearts are then "taken captive by their eyes and ears." They seek after action, and fall victims to the first evil counsellor they meet, or the first gust of passion which assails them. But the truly brave man must be righteous and benevolent; he must act up to what he believes to be right;[3] and must be calm in face of adversity. It has been said that it requires greater courage in a soldier to run away in battle than to face the enemy, and Confucius seems to have been of this opinion, for

Le ke.   [2] Lun yu, xvii. 23.   [3] Ibid. ii. 24.

he says, To possess the feeling of shame is akin to valour.[1]

According to Confucius, benevolence is a leading characteristic of perfect virtue, for it is the root of righteousness,[2] inasmuch as it is the complete virtue of the original heart. By it all relations of society are maintained. The superior man, who is the embodiment of benevolence, cherishes the people by means of it,[3] and it finds its highest development in the attachment of relatives.[4] But it extends its humanizing influences beyond the circle of friends, and outside the relations existing between governors and those they govern. The whole human race should be the recipients of it, and as Han Fei-tsze says, benevolence is to love men out of a sincere heart gladly, or, as Confucius said, benevolence is to love all men. The great enemy with which benevolence has naturally to contend is selfishness. It is difficult to be benevolent in the midst of selfish desires, says the Le ke, but at the same time it may be used as a lever by which covetousness may be overcome. But it is plain that true benevolence cannot exist side by side with selfishness ; for just as matured benignity is the root, and respectful earnestness is the ground of benevolence, so is noble-minded generosity the result of it.[5] Self must be conquered before a man can be truly benevolent. Dignity, said Confucius, is near to propriety, moderation to benevolence, and faithfulness to love.

---

[1] Chung yung, xx. 10.
[2] Le ke.
[3] Yih king. K'een kwa.
[4] Chung yung, xx. 5.
[5] Le ke.

But benevolence should be exercised with discretion, and should not be only the result of the impulses of the moment. "If a benevolent man," asked a disciple of Confucius, "should be told that there is a man in the well, I suppose he will go in after him?" "Why should he?" answered the Sage. "A superior man may be induced to go to the well, but he cannot be made to go down into it. He may be imposed upon, but he cannot be befooled."[1] But though benevolence is nigh to all who seek after it, there are instances in which superior men have been lacking in it; but on the contrary, no mean man was ever known to possess it.[2] But to superior men, as a rule, its possession is beyond measure valuable. On no occasion will they act contrary to it. In moments of haste they cleave to it, and in seasons of danger they cling to it.[3]

The opposing front which selfishness shows to benevolence makes it, however, difficult for the scholar to practise that virtue. Selfishness is a heavy weight upon him, and is one from which the grave alone releases him.[4] But sufficient for their need is the strength of all who really strive after benevolence. Unfortunately, selfishness is more powerful in most men's minds than benevolence, and few shake off that which sits so lightly on them for that which is so difficult to bear. "Benevolence," said Confucius, "is more to man than either water or fire. And yet, though I have seen men die from treading on water and fire, I have never seen a man

---

[1] Lun yu, vi. 24.   [2] Ibid. xiv. 7.
[3] Ibid. iv. 5, 3.   [4] Ibid. viii. 2.

die from treading the course of benevolence."[1] But some men struggle to attain it, and yet fail in the pursuit. Even Confucius declined to rank himself as a perfectly benevolent man.[1]

There are, however, various degrees of benevolence. There is the benevolence of the sage, there is the benevolence of the wise man, there is the benevolence of the virtuous man, and there is the benevolence of a hypocrite. Benevolence enables the sage to know heaven and to use the seasons, to know earth and to use its wealth, to know man and to pacify and please him. But the benevolent hypocrite is only outwardly moderate and ceremonially clean. When disorder arises, he is unable to regulate it, and he does nothing to rectify vice and backslidings. Though he live in the village lane, he is as if sitting in mire and charcoal. When ordered to appear at court, he professes himself ready to go through fire and water. But he gives employment to none but his own people, and won't taste any but his own food. He disturbs the age, and thinks lightly of death. His brothers he neglects, and all his schemes turn out ill-omened. Such is a hypocrite's benevolence; but, on the other hand, "if the will be set on (true) benevolence, there will be no practice of wickedness."[2]

But rightly to understand all that Confucius meant by benevolence, we must consider the different qualities which he taught were embraced in that virtue. These were reciprocity, loyalty, reverence, and faith. The first two being so nearly allied are always treated

---

[1] Lun yu, vii. 33. [2] Ibid. iv. 4.

together by Chinese philosophers. Reciprocity, they say, is born of loyalty ; and, again, loyalty is the root and reciprocity is the branch ; loyalty is the substance, reciprocity the shadow.[1] In explaining what he meant by reciprocity, Confucius found it easier to describe it by showing what is not reciprocity. As when a sovereign who is incapable of transacting business expects his ministers to serve him ; a man who is incapable of filial piety expects his son to acknowledge his indebtedness to him ; a brother who is incapable of respect expects his younger brother to show him deference. These severally do not display reciprocity.[2] To put oneself in the place of another is reciprocity, and to devote oneself entirely is loyalty.[3]

To devote oneself entirely to the performance of one's duties, said Confucius, is loyalty, and thus this virtue enters into every relation of life. There is no position in which this self-sacrificing devotion may not be displayed, but the term more especially applies to the higher kinds of devotion, notably patriotism. But ministers should serve their prince loyally,[4] people their sovereign,[5] and even kings their subjects.[6] Men should loyally discharge their duties to their fellow-men,[7] and friends should loyally admonish one another in times of difficulty and temptation.[8] But there is a limit to this last display of loyalty. "Loyally admonish your friend, and kindly try to lead him," said

---

[1] Sing le.
[2] Kung-tsze kea yu.
[3] Kung-tsze kea yu.
[4] Lun yu, iii. 19.
[5] Ibid. ii. 20.
[6] Chung yung, xx. 14.
[7] Lun yu, i. 4.
[8] Ibid. xii. 23.

Confucius. "If, however, you find him impracticable, stop. Do not disgrace yourself." But the great end of loyalty should be to benefit the object of it. "Can there be loyalty which does not lead to the instruction of its object?"[1] remarked Confucius; and thus it is doubly blessed, blessing both him that gives and him that takes. Though we are told in the *Kung-tsze kea yu* that loyalty is akin to sincerity, it is not always the sign of perfect virtue. For instance, we find Tsze-chang asking: "The minister Tsze-wǎn thrice took office and manifested no joy in his countenance, and as often retired from office without showing any displeasure. He also made it a point to inform the new minister of the way in which he had conducted the government. What do you say of him?" The Master replied, "He was loyal." "Was he perfectly virtuous?" again inquired the disciple. "I do not know," said the Sage. "How can he be pronounced perfectly virtuous?"[2] But though loyalty may exist without perfect virtue, perfect virtue cannot exist without loyalty. Without it patriotism would cease to exist, and every high and noble deed would be marred by the obtrusion of self-interest, of which loyalty is the abnegation.

Much as loyalty is allied to reciprocity, so is dignity akin to reverence. It is the outward display of the reverence which finds its home in the heart. It is by reverence that the superior man preserves internal rectitude, and by righteousness that he maintains an outward regularity of conduct.[3] As we might expect

Lun yu, xiv. 8.   [2] Ibid. v. 18,
[3] Yih king. K'wan kwa,

to learn from Confucius, reverence finds its highest employment in paying dutiful respect to one's parents. Not the mere perfunctory observance of the ordinary duties, "for dogs and horses are able to do something in this way,"[1] but with true reverence, as to the author of one's being, to serve and obey them. Next to parents, all superiors should be the objects of reverence. Ministers should reverently discharge their duties to their prince, and even the sovereign finds a superior in heaven to which his attitude should be reverent. "Heaven," says the Shoo-king, "hears and sees as our people hear and see; Heaven highly approves and displays its terrors as our people approve and would awe—such a connection there is between the upper and lower worlds. How reverent ought the master of the earth to be."[2] But he should also approach his duties as a ruler with reverent solicitude. "In my relations to the millions of the people," said T'ai-k'ang, "I should feel as much anxiety as if I were driving six horses with rotten reins. How reverent ought the ruler of men to be."[3] But this reverence must be reciprocal, and to a certain extent conditional. A sovereign may only claim the reverence of his subjects when he rules them with gravity and propriety, in which case it becomes his due; but he forfeits all right to it when he ceases to be a minister of God for good.

The spirits also are fitting objects of reverence, though Confucius, with his intuitive dislike of the

[1] Lun yu, ii. 7. [2] Shoo-king. Kaou-yaou mow.
[3] Shoo-king. Woo-tsze che ko.

I

supernatural, recommended all wise men, while show-ing them respect, to keep aloof from them.[1] And lastly, reverence is due from man to man. " Let the superior man never fail reverently to order his con-duct, and let him be respectful to others, and obser-vant of propriety, then all within the four seas will be his brethren."

All the qualities mentioned above find their com-plement in faithfulness. Without it they are nothing worth, and must degenerate into hollow hypocrisies. Faithfulness is the foundation of conduct,[2] and is as necessary to truly virtuous conduct as a boat is to a man wishing to cross a river, or as oars are to a boat. A man may wish to be good, but if he has not estab-lished his conduct by faithfulness, he is like a man without a boat, or a boat without oars.[3] With such faithfulness the learned should clothe themselves as with armour.[4] " Hold faithfulness and sincerity as first principles,"[5] said Confucius ; and the earnestness with which he insists on this, repeating the same in-junction over and over again, is a point in his teach-ing which is well worthy of admiration. " I do not know," said he, " how a man is to get on without faithfulness. How can a carriage be made to go with-out the cross-bar for yoking the oxen to, or a small carriage without the arrangement for yoking the horses ? "[6]

And if faithfulness is so essential among men

---

[1] Lun yu, vi. 20 ; xii. 5, 4.　　　[2] Sin lun.
[3] Sin lun.　　　　　　　　　　　[4] Le ke.
[5] Lun yu, ix. 24.　　　　　　　　[6] Ibid. ii. 22.

generally, more especially is it so between friends and between the governed and the governors. The philosopher Tsăng said that he examined himself daily to inquire whether he had been faithful to his friends,[1] and even more important is it that rulers should act faithfully towards their subjects. The word of a sovereign must instantly pass as true coin among his people, or they will cease to reverence him, and will turn with contempt from his instructions. " To rule a country of a thousand chariots," said Confucius, " there must be reverent attention to business, and faithfulness, economy in expenditure, and love for the people."

By faithfulness in the above sense, Confucius meant sincerity, but in one or two passages in Confucian literature there seems to be a higher meaning attached to it, which would seem to imply a faith in a superintending providence. " When a man does not seek after that which he desires," says the Le-ke, " and yet obtains it, he exercises faith." And again Mencius says : "If a superior man has not faith, how can he take a firm hold on things ? " But these exceptions are overborne by the weight of every other reference, which point conclusively to the propriety of translating the word *Sin* by faithfulness rather than by faith.

The man who has developed all these virtues, and thus has cultivated his person, is considered competent to rule a family. In the family, Confucius recognized the concentration of those relations which

---

[1] Lun yu, i. 4.

exist in the State. The same virtues are required in the head of the family as in the ruler of a kingdom, and the same respectful reverence should be paid by the children to the father as is due from the subjects to the sovereign. A man, therefore, who can rule a family can govern a state. As master of a household he is the representative of Heaven, and the prototype of sovereigns. "Heaven and earth existing," says the Yih king, "all things exist; all things existing, then male and female exist; male and female existing, then the relation of husband and wife exists; from the existence of man and wife follows the relation of father and son; father and son existing, then prince and minister exist; prince and minister existing, then upper and lower classes; upper and lower classes existing, decorum and propriety are interchanged."[1]

"It is not possible," said Confucius in the "Great Learning," "for a man to teach others who cannot teach his own family. Therefore a ruler, without going beyond his family, completes the lessons for the State. There is filial piety; therewith the sovereign should be served. There is fraternal submission, with which the elders and superiors should be served. There is kindness, with which the multitude should be treated. . . . From the loving example of one family the whole State becomes loving; and from its courtesies, the whole State becomes courteous; while, from the ambition and perverseness of one man, the whole State may be led to rebellious disorder—such is the nature of influence." This verifies

---

[1] Yih king. Seu kwa chuen.

the saying: "Affairs may be ruined by a single sentence; a kingdom may be settled by one man. Yaou and Shun led on the people by benevolence, and the people followed them. Keĕ and Show led on the empire with violence, and the people followed them. The orders which these issued were contrary to the practice which they loved, and so the people did not obey them. On this account the ruler must himself be possessed of the good qualities, and then he may require them in the people. . . . Thus we see how the government of the State depends on the regulation of the family."

In the Book of Poetry it is said: "That peach-tree, so delicate and elegant! How luxuriant is its foliage! This girl is going to her husband's house. She will rightly order her household." Let the household be rightly ordered, and then the people of the State may be taught. In the Book of Poetry it is also said: "They can discharge their duties to their elder brothers. They can discharge their duties to their younger brothers." Let the ruler discharge his duties to his elder and younger brothers, and then he may teach the people of the State.

Again, in the Book of Poetry it is written: "In his deportment there is nothing wrong; he rectifies all the people of the State." Yes, when the ruler, as a father, a son, and a brother is a model, then the people imitate him.

We have already considered the excellencies which should distinguish the superior man, and by the exercise of which he should rule his household, and it now therefore only remains for us to review the virtue which should be displayed by his family in their relation towards him. And the first of all virtues, whether in a son or in a subject, is filial piety. It is this which distinguishes man from brutes; it is this which recognizes the true relation between child and parent, between father and heaven; and it is by the exercise of this, therefore, that the harmony of the universe is preserved. This idea was not originated by Confucius, it had obtained a firm hold of the national mind many centuries before his time. "As an example of love," said E-yin to King Ching, "it is for you to love your elders; and as an example of respect, it is for you to respect your relations. The commencement is in the family and State; the consummation is in the empire."[1] Again, King Ching, addressing his minister, said: "Fung, such chief criminals (as you have described) are greatly to be abhorred, but how much more detestable are the unfilial and unbrotherly. As, for example, the son who does not reverently discharge his duty to his father, but greatly wounds his father's heart, causing him thereby to hate him; or the younger brother who is neglectful of the manifest will of Heaven, and refuses to respect his elder brother, so that his elder brother does not think of the toil of his parents in bringing him up, and is unbrotherly to his junior. If we who are charged with the government do not treat persons who proceed to such wickedness as offenders, the laws of our nature bestowed by Heaven on our people will be thrown into disorder or

[1] Shoo-king. E-heun.

destroyed. You must deal speedily with such persons according to the penal laws of King Wăn (12th century B.C.), punishing severely and sparing not."[1]

The King Wăn here referred to in the course of an address against the use of spirituous liquors, makes an exception in favour of those who show filial piety to their parents. "Ye people of the land of Mei," he said, "if you busily employ yourselves in cultivating your millet, and hastening about it in the service of your fathers and elders, and if with your carts and oxen you traffic to a distance, that you may be able filially to supply the wants of your parents; then when your parents are happy, you may set forth your spirits clear and strong and use them."[2] Confucius was then acting the part of a transmitter when he said : "Filial piety and fraternal submission ! are they not the root of all benevolent actions?"[3]

But what does filial piety consist in? According to Confucius it consists in obedience; in serving one's parents when alive according to propriety; in burying them when dead according to propriety; and in sacrificing to them according to propriety.[4] These outlines are filled up in other places with most minute details as to the conduct of sons, which should be such as not to cause their parents any anxiety beyond that arising from their illnesses.[5] During the lifetime of his parents a son should not go abroad; or if he do so, then to a fixed place. When at home, he should rise with the first cock-

[1] Shoo-king. K'ang kaou.   [2] Shoo-king. Tsew kaou.
[3] Lun yu, i. 2, 2.   [4] Ibid. ii. 5, 3.
[5] Ibid. ii. 6.

crow, and having washed and dressed himself carefully should inquire what the wishes of his parents are as to the food they would eat and drink. He should not enter a room unless invited by his father, nor retire without permission; neither should he speak unless spoken to. When leaving the house, he should report himself, and on returning should make his presence known. He should be regular in his amusements, attentive to his calling, constant in speech, and avoiding all reference to old age.[1] This last is a point strongly insisted upon, and every boy has held up to him as an example to be followed the conduct of Laou Lai-tsze, who, fearing that the recognition by his parents of the fact that he was seventy years old would remind them of their own great age, used to dress himself in a child's frock and play about the room like an infant!

The highest form of filial piety is then that shown towards parents, for whom every dutiful son must entertain the deepest affection. This being so, it follows naturally that he will wait upon them with a gladsome countenance and a pleasing manner. Recognizing that his body is inherited from his parents, he will love them as part of his own self, and will shrink as much from doing anything likely to bring discredit on them, as from anything calculated to ruin his own good name. "Of all things," said Confucius, "which derive their natures from heaven and earth, man is the most noble; and of all the duties which are incumbent on him, there is none

---

[1] Le ke.

greater than filial obedience; nor in performing this is there anything so essential as to reverence one's father; and as a mark of reverence there is nothing more important than to place him on an equality with heaven. Thus did the noble lord of Chow. Formerly he sacrificed on the round altar to the spirits of his remote ancestors, as equal with heaven; and in the open hall he sacrificed to Wăn Wang (his father) as equal with Shang-te." This is one of the innumerable passages which enjoin the duty of ancestral worship. Confucius was less emphatic on this point than many of the earlier sages of whose teachings he described himself as being a transmitter, but the principle runs through the whole of the Confucian system, and is intimately bound up with it. Confucianism must be torn up by the roots before it will be logically possible for the Chinese to make light of a duty which springs from one of the most generous instincts of the human heart, and which is bound up with everything that is good in the constitution of the Chinese commonwealth.

But while it is incumbent on a son to obey the wishes of his parents, it is also part of his duty to remonstrate with them should they act contrary to the rules of propriety. But any such remonstrances must be made humbly and with bated breath ; and should these on the first occasion fail to effect their object, they may be repeated three times. Beyond this a dutiful son will not press his reproofs, but will mourn in silence the obduracy of his parents. When sickness befalls them, he must not only double his attentions to them, but he should display his grief by leaving his cap tassel uncombed, by not walking abroad, by abstaining from tasty food and choice wine, from playing music, and from loud laughter.[1]

At their death he must give them the obsequies befitting their rank,[2] and since a son is "fostered by his parents for three years"[3] he should mourn for them for the same period. And his respect should teach him to preserve the customs of his father for the same time. The sacrifices at the tombs should be provided with no niggard hand and should be offered with a full consciousness of the presence of the dead.[4]

But filial piety is due to others besides parents. It commands the minister to serve his prince loyally; the Mandarin to perform the duties of his office reverently; the friend to be faithful to his friend; and the soldier to be brave in battle.[5] But it spreads even beyond this. "Every tree," says the Le-ke, "has its appointed time to perish, and every beast its appointed time to die, and he who cuts down a tree or kills an animal before their time is guilty of unfilial conduct."[6]

Viewing with such supreme importance the duty of filial piety, it is only natural that the State should visit with condign punishment those who are guilty of any dereliction of it. The heaviest penalties of the law have always been exacted in such cases and the Peking Gazette of 1877 contains mention of five culprits, one of whom was a lunatic, who were sliced to death for the murder of their parents.

---

[1] Le ke.
[2] Chung yung, xviii. 3.
[3] Lun yu, xvii. 21, 6.
[4] Ibid. xix. 5.
[5] Le ke.
[6] Ibid.

"Filial piety," said Confucius, "is the beginning of virtue, and brotherly love is the sequel of virtue." One is the natural consequence of the other, just as filial piety follows on the display of sympathy from the parents. It is brotherly love which unites members of a household together, and which with filial piety is the root of all benevolent actions. "Happy union," says the Book of Poetry, "with wife and children is like the music of lutes and harps. And when there is concord among brethren the harmony is delightful and enduring." There is no friend like a brother. He springs from the same source as yourself, and was nourished at the same breasts. These were the considerations which knit together the hearts of brethren "in the brave days of old." Then brothers loved to dwell together under the same roof, and to lie beside each other in the same tomb. But nowadays Chinese. moralists complain that the love for wife and children surpasses that between brethren. "I have heard," says a well-known writer, "of brothers living asunder, but I never see man and wife living apart." And yet how much more sacred should be the bond, forged by Heaven, which unites brothers, than that which, being the work of man, binds together husband and wife.[1] The love which brother should bear to brother is second only to that which is due from children to parents. It consists in mutual friendship, joyful harmony, and dutiful obedience on the part of the younger to the elder brother.

[1] Ta tae Le ke, and commentaries.

No step in life should be taken by a younger son without first consulting with his father and elder brothers, and in return for the sympathy and affection shown him, he should open his whole heart unreservedly to them. In all things the younger must show deference to the elder brother, and must give way to him in everything, whether in speaking or in walking, in sitting down and rising up. On the other hand, elder brothers must show a good example to their juniors. "The posterity of the Sage Confucius, it is stated, are never known to be angry; and the posterity of Tsăng-tsze, one of the Sage's most distinguished disciples, are never known to revile others."[1] And this is as it should be, for are not brothers of the same flesh and bones; and is not, therefore, a slight put upon a brother really a slight put upon the parents?[2]

The very inferior position held by women in China from time immemorial deprives them of all right to fraternal regard. A slavish submission is a woman's highest duty, and no better description can be given of the various fates awaiting sons and daughters than that quoted below from the Book of Poetry, where the poet forecasts the future of King Seuen :[3]—

" Sons shall be his " (the king's), "on couches lulled to rest.
The little ones, enrobed, with sceptres play ;
Their infant cries are loud as stern behests ;
Their knees the vermeil covers shall display.
As king hereafter one shall be addressed ;
The rest our Princes, all the states shall sway."

----

[1] Dr. Legge's Lectures on Imperial Confucianism.
[2] Ibid.   [3] Dr. Legge's version of the Book of Odes.

" And daughters also to him shall be born.
  They shall be placed upon the ground to sleep ;
  Their playthings tiles, their dress the simplest worn ;
  Their part alike from good and ill to keep,
  And ne'er their parents' hearts to cause to mourn ;
  To cook his food, and spirit malt to keep."

It is only when a woman becomes a mother that she receives the respect which is by right due to her, and then the inferiority of her sex disappears before the requirements of filial love, which is the crown and glory of China.

But at the root of all family ties is the relation of husband and wife,[1] which is as the relation of heaven and earth. On this subject Confucius was singularly silent, possibly because his own married life was unhappy. A man who is compelled to divorce his wife is not likely to take a favourable view of women in general, and thus we find that Confucius looked on women as necessary evils, who were to be endured only as the possible mothers of men. " Of all people," remarked the Sage, " women and servants are the most difficult to manage. If you are familiar with them, they become forward, and if you keep them at a distance, they become discontented."[2] For conjugal fidelity on the part of the husband he had no overweening respect, and speaks in one passage with contempt of the " small fidelity" of common men who are bound to one wife.[3] But on the other hand, he inveighs repeatedly against indulgence in lustful pleasures, and when the Duke of Ts'e sent a present of female musicians to the ruler of Loo, Confucius

[1] Le ke.   [2] Lun yu, xvii. 25.   [3] Ibid. xiv. 18, 2.

marked his disapprobation of the reception given them by withdrawing from the court. "A woman," he said, disparagingly, "is unable to stand alone, and therefore when young depends on her father and brothers, when married, on her husband, and after his death, on her sons."[1]

The great object of marriage is to beget children, and especially sons, who may perform the required sacrifices at the tombs of their parents. And on this account it is fit and proper for a childless widower to take to himself a second wife, while as no such reason exists for the re-marriage of a widow, it is an act of lewdness on her part again to enter the bonds of matrimony. To such a length is this desire for children carried, that barrenness forms one of the "seven reasons for divorce" sanctioned by Confucius. These seven reasons are as follows :—1. Disobedience to her father-in-law or mother-in-law; 2. Barrenness ; 3. Lewdness ; 4. Jealousy ; 5. Leprosy ; 6. Garrulousness ; and 7. Stealing.[2]

Such a law necessarily places the wife much in the power of the husband, and it is her interest, therefore, as well as her duty, to pay him due reverence in all things ; to be courteous, humble, and conciliatory in her address and manner towards him, and to obey without question his every word. If his conduct should be in any way contrary to right principles, she may gently remonstrate with him, but not so as to irritate or annoy him.[3] In this way domestic harmony is maintained ; but if a husband and wife

---

[1] Le ke. [2] Ta Tae le. [3] Seun tsze.

regard one another with rebellious eyes, the household soon falls into disorder.[1] According to the Confucian system, a woman's life is divided into periods of seven months or years, and a man's into periods of eight months or years. Thus an infant girl cuts her teeth at seven months, and changes them at seven years; at fourteen she arrives at puberty, and at seventy she should be prepared to die. A boy, on the other hand, cuts his teeth at eight months, changes them at eight years, arrives at puberty at sixteen, and has exhausted life by the age of eighty.

Fifteen, therefore, is a marriageable age for a woman, and twenty for a man. This is about the proportion of age that should be maintained between man and wife. An old man marrying a young girl is like a decayed willow-tree producing buds, and cannot but end in disaster. It is, however, one degree better than an old woman marrying a young husband, which is like a decayed willow tree producing blossoms, and is in every way detestable.[2]

It follows from what has been said that Confucius, like the Jewish lawgivers, fully sanctioned polygamy, and with the same object. No Jewish patriarch ever longed for a son more ardently than do Chinamen, and so legitimate is the desire considered, that it is regarded as a matter of course that the husband of a childless wife should take a concubine to raise up seed to himself. If, however, the possession of descendants is looked upon as important in the case of

[1] Yih king. Seaou chuh kwa.   Yih king, Ta kwo kwa.

private individuals, it is *à fortiori* important that the Emperor should have an heir to succeed him, and it is consequently decreed by the "Rites of the Chow Dynasty" that to insure him against the chance of being childless, he should be provided with three concubines of the first class, nine of the second, twenty-seven of the third, and eighty-one of the fourth, besides the Empress. The evils which flow from this imperial system are so obvious as scarcely to require mention, and not unfrequently defeat their own object, while the introduction of concubines into private households is a fruitful source of great misery. The failure to recognize the sanctity of the marriage bond is a great blot in the Confucian system. It has, in a great measure, destroyed domesticity, it has robbed women of their lawful influence, and has degraded them into a position which is little better than slavery. "Men being firm by nature," said Seun-tsze, "are virtuous, and women being soft, are useful." This saying justly represents the estimate commonly held of the relative standing of the two sexes.

"Husband and wife," said Choo He, "is the heaven-ordained relation on which depends succession, and friendship is the heaven-ordained relationship on which depends the correction of one's character. For by it the way of men is traced out, and men's highest principles are built up." Confucius and his followers have laid great stress upon the importance of friendship, and if their advice were always followed in the choice of friends, no doubt the great results they expect from it would frequently ensue. If, for example, men were only to associate with those who, being of one mind and pursuing the same ends as themselves, are virtuous and upright, standing firm in righteousness, the world would be a great deal better than it is.[1] And here, as at every point, Confucius fails to give any reason why men should choose the virtuous course rather than the opposite. It is true he says that "To find enjoyment in many worthy friends is advantageous;"[2] and again, "There are three advantageous kinds of friendship—viz., with the upright, with the sincere, and with the experienced; and there are three injurious kinds of friendship—viz., with the haughty, with the coxcomb, and with the glib-tongued."[3] But he holds out no other reason why men should seek their friends among the good. A high value is, however, set on true friendship.

"From the Emperor downwards all must have friends. Friendship is the first of the social relationships, and may not be abandoned for a single day."[4] No one should have a friend who is not equal to himself;[5] and the best friends are those which a dutiful son inherits from his father.[6] Such friends, whether in trouble or sorrow, are always welcome. They halve one's cares and double one's joys. They are wealth to the poor, strength to the weak, and medicine to the sick.[7] They are ever ready to forget one's ill-treatment of them, and to remember one's

[1] Le ke.
[2] Lun yu, xvi. 5.
[3] Ibid. xvi. 4.
[4] Choo tsze yu luy.
[5] Lun yu, i. 8, 3.
[6] Sing le. [7] Ibid

K

virtues, and whether near or at a distance, they neither suspect nor doubt one.[1]

Literature is a bond which unites friends in the truest friendship. The superior man gains friends by literary exertions, and enhances his humanity by friendship. "When you are living in a state," said Confucius, "take service with the most worthy among the great officers, and make friends of the most virtuous among the scholars."[2] A man should behave to his friend as he would have his friend behave towards him.[3] He should faithfully admonish him, and kindly try to lead him. But if he find him impracticable, he should stop, lest he disgrace himself.[4] He should, like the disciple Tsze-loo, desire to have chariots and horses and light fur dresses that he might share them with his friends.[5] Whenever a friend of Confucius died who had no relations to perform the necessary funeral rites, he buried him, considering this to be one of the bounden duties of friendship. In the same way he never acknowledged any present made him by a friend, excepting the flesh of sacrifice, which having been offered by his friend to the spirits of his parents or ancestors, required acknowledgment.[6]

Above all things, there should be entire confidence between friends. To conceal resentment and appear as a friend is a shame,[7] and destroys that sincerity which is his mark of true friendship. "He who is

[1] Kea yu.
[2] Lun yu, xv. 9.
[3] Chung yung, xiii. 4.
[4] Lun yu, xii. 23.
[5] Ibid. v. 25.
[6] Ibid. x. 15.
[7] Ibid. v. 24.

not trusted by his friends," said Confucius, 'will not gain the confidence of his sovereign. . . . . He that is not obedient to his parents, will not be trusted by his friends."[1]

[1] Chung yung, xx. 17.

CHAPTER V.

THE GOVERNMENT OF THE STATE.

THIS is the next stage at which the superior man arrives. Having learnt to rule well his household, he is able to govern the empire. And here he first comes into direct relationship with "the way of heaven and earth," which is to be perfected by his development of the nature of men and things, in order that he may "cherish the people."[1] The good of the people is the main object of good government. "No virtue," said Emperor Kuh (2435 B.C.), "is higher than to love all men, and there is no loftier aim in government than to profit all men."[2] When Confucius was asked what should be done for the people, he replied, "Enrich them;" and when asked what more should be done, he answered, "Teach them."[3] Few would be inclined to dissent from the view that it would be advantageous to the State if the people were sufficiently well off and efficiently instructed. But here, again, we have to find fault with the very impractical nature of the advice offered by the Sage. He does not attempt to explain how

---

[1] Yih king. Tai kwa.   [2] Shoo king.
[3] Lun yu, xiii. 9

he would propose to enrich the people, but seems lost in a dream in which were to be revived the days of Yaou and Shun, as described in the Shoo-king, when by the force of their individual characters evil was blotted out from the empire, and with it poverty and ignorance. "If any one of the princes would employ me," was his vain boast, "I would accomplish something considerable in the course of a twelvemonth, and in three years the government would be perfected."[1]

All his advice on the science of government is borrowed from the Shoo-king, and, as is often the case under such circumstances, loses some of its completeness in the transfer. We there read that virtue is seen in the goodness of government, and that the government is tested by its nourishing the people.[2] Confucius said: "The requisites of government are, that there be sufficiency of food, sufficiency of military equipment, and the confidence of the people in their rulers."[3] This is only an imperfect abstract of the passage in the Shoo-king, which he probably had in his mind at the moment. There we are told that the eight requisites of government are—Food, trade, the maintenance of the appointed sacrifices, the Ministry of Works, the Ministry of Instruction, the Ministry of Crime, arrangements for the entertainment of guests from afar, and provision for the support of the army.[4] Here we have a much more complete picture of the machinery of govern-

---

[1] Lun yu, xiii. 10.   [2] Shoo-king. Ta yu mow.
[3] Lun yu, xii. 7.   [4] Shoo-king. Hung fan.

ment. For we have indicated the sources from which
food for the people is to be derived, and the means
by which their moral welfare is to be maintained,
their comfort and education are to be promoted, the
law-abiding are to be protected from the lawless, the
friendship of neighbouring states is to be encouraged,
and the national honour is to be supported.

In denying to Confucius the credit of originality,
we are merely accepting his own estimate of his
teaching. Almost all his doctrines, and certainly his
most striking utterances, are borrowed from the earlier
classics, and, as a rule, the impression on the original
coin is more deeply cut than on the reproduction.
Nowhere does Confucius give such radical advice on
the science of government as that offered by the
great Yu to his sovereign : "Attend to the springs of
things, and study stability."[1]   Of the conditions
under which good government will exist, and of the
results of it, he has plenty to say. According to him,
good government exists when the prince is prince,
and the minister is minister ; when the father is father,
and the son is son.[2] This is all true enough; but
Yu struck deeper when he said, "When a sovereign
can realize the difficulty of his sovereignty, and the
minister can realize the difficulty of his ministry,
government will be well ordered."[3]

In order that government should be stable, it is
necessary that it should be conducted on virtuous principles ; and to this end it is imperative not only that

---

[1] Shoo-king. Ta yu mow.   [2] Lun yu, xii. 11, 2.
[3] Shoo-king. Ta yu mow.

the sovereign should be upright in all things, but that nepotism in the distribution of offices should be strictly avoided, and that only men of worth and ability should be employed.   Such conduct will draw down on the land the gifts of Shang-te, and the blessings of Heaven, adds Yu.[1]   Confucius has no such heavenly rewards to offer.   His essentially pagan mind rejected the idea of any spiritual interference in the affairs of men.   He would have men virtuous for virtue's sake; and he attempted to impose on the ever-varying natures of men a moral system which he felt was sufficient for the guidance of his own steps, and which he therefore imagined would satisfy the spiritual wants of his fellow-citizens.   This mistake of Confucius has been shared in by men of every age and of every clime; but if ever it was justified by results, it was so in his case.   Opinions which in other countries have been confined to a comparative few, have in China been adopted by the nation at large for more than three-and-twenty centuries.

The force of example is one of the leading doctrines of Confucianism.   If the sovereign is desirous of doing good, the people will be good ; and if the ruler be not covetous, even though he were to reward the people to steal, they would be honest,[2] said the Sage.   Few will deny the immense power of example. " Dead flies cause the ointment of the apothecary to send forth a stinking savour," wrote Solomon ; and the experience of every day teaches how potent is the force of example for good or for bad in every con-

---

[1] Shoo-king.   [2] Lun yu, xii. 18, 19.

dition of life—in the school, the household, the pro-
fession, and society. But Confucius carried the
doctrine to an absurd length in the face of every true
lesson of history, and of the events of his own
career.

Much, however, that Confucius taught on the
subject of government may be quoted without
criticism. In reply to Tsze-chang's question, How
should a sovereign act in order that he may govern
properly? he replied: Let him honour the five
excellent, and banish the four bad things. . . . .
(The five good things are)—(1) When the person
in authority is beneficent without great expenditure;
that is, when he makes more beneficial to his
people the things from which they naturally derive
benefit: (2) When he lays tasks on the people
without their repining; that is, when he chooses
the labours which are proper, and employs them
on them: (3) When he pursues what he desires
without being covetous; that is, when his desires
are set on benevolent government, and he realizes
it: (4) When he maintains a dignified ease without
being proud; that is, whether he has to do with
many people or with few, or with great things or with
small, he does not dare to show any disrespect:
(5) When he is majestic without being fierce; that
is, when he adjusts his clothes and cap, and throws a
dignity into his looks, so that, thus dignified, he is
looked at with awe. (The four bad things are :)—(1)
To put the people to death without having instructed
them;—this is called cruelty. To require from them
suddenly the full tale of work without having given

them warning ;—this is called oppression. To issue orders as if without urgency, at first, and when the time comes, to insist upon them with severity ;—this is called injury. And, generally speaking, to give pay or rewards to men, and yet to do it in a stingy way ; —this is called acting the part of a mere official.[1]

Next, then, to the character of the sovereign the characters of the officials employed by him are most essential. As we learn from the Shoo-king, good and bad governments depend upon the various officers.[2] Confucius reiterated this dictum, and enlarged on the necessity of employing only men of virtue and talents. " With the right men," he added, " the growth of government is rapid, just as vegetation is rapid in the earth ; and indeed their government might be called an easily growing rush. Therefore the administration of government lies in getting proper men. Such men are to be got by means of the ruler's own character. That character is to be cultivated by his treading in the ways of duty. And the teaching those ways of duty is to be cultivated by the cherishing of benevolence."[3] Under such an administration the criterion of good government quoted by Confucius may be safely applied. Those who are near will be made happy, and those who are far off will be attracted.[4] By " those who are far off " it must not be supposed that Confucius had in his mind any but those neighbouring tribes who would naturally be so struck with the contrast between their

[1] Lun yu, xx. 2.   [2] Shoo-king. Shwŏ ming-chung.
[3] Chung yung, xx. 2, 3.   [4] Lun yu, xiii. 16, 2.

own rude laws and the carefully modelled govern-ment of the empire, that they would be willing to acknowledge themselves the subjects of China.

Of the officials of his own time he speaks, not un-naturally considering how they scorned his teachings, with supreme contempt. "Pooh!" said he, "they are so many jackanapes, not worthy to be taken into account."[1] Nothing is so trying to baffled virtue as successful charlatanism, and Confucius was not above venting his spleen against those who rode in the high places of the earth. In contrast with such, he de-scribed three degrees of competent officials, the first and best being those who in their conduct maintained a sense of shame, and who, when sent to any quarter, do not disgrace their Sovereign's commission; the next are those whom their relatives pronounce to be filial, and their clansmen pronounce to be fraternal; and the last are those who are determined to be sincere in what they say, and to carry out what they devise. "These are obstinate little men," adds the sage.[2]

It will be seen that in government, as with every-thing else, Confucius strove with all his might to carry his countrymen back to the ideal times of kings Wăn and Woo. He refused to recognize the changes which were foreshadowed by the growth of new and vigorous states, and by the decrepitude of the Imperial Kingdom of Chow, and attempted to bolster up that which was already falling to pieces, and to suppress the aspirations of those who, as must

---

[1] Lun yu, xiii. 20, 4.   [2] Ibid. xiii. 20, 1-3.

have been obvious to every one but himself, were destined to fight for the mastery over the ruins of the royal house.   The sum of his teachings may be described in his own words : " Follow the seasons of Hea.   Ride in the state chariots of Yin.   Wear the ceremonial cap of Chow.   Let the music be the Shaou, with its pantomimes.   Banish the Songs of Ch'ing, and keep far from specious talkers."[1]

The two motive powers of government, according to Confucius, are righteousness and the observance of ceremonies, and the presence or absence of these find their expression in the music of the period. " The superior man by respect preserves internal uprightness, and by rectitude outward propriety of conduct,"[2] wrote the Duke of Chow.   Righteousness is the law of the world, as ceremonies form a rule to the heart.[3]   It was essential that in a system such as that of Confucius, which was based on the relations of man to man, a full and exact code of ceremonies should be established to mark the degrees of reverence which were due to the various degrees of kindred and ranks in life.   In this way the near and distant relationships were settled, suspicions and doubts were decided, the similar and dissimilar were plainly distinguished, and the true was separated from the false.[4]   But ceremonies, as employed by Confucius, were intended to play a more important part even than this.   They were to keep all unruly passions in check.   They were to produce a uniform reverential manner among all classes of the people.   Sons of all

---

[1] Lun yu, xv. x. 2–6.   [2] Yih king.   K'wan kwa.
[3] Shoo-king.   [4] Le ke.

ranks and degrees were to conform to exactly the same elaborate ceremonials towards their parents; officials and people were to observe strictly the rules of etiquette laid down for their guidance, and thus by means of ceremonies the people were to be educated to play their part as members of the household and the State. There can be no doubt that the observance of ceremonies has a pacifying effect. It is difficult to fall out violently by the way, with a man to whom one has been taught all one's life to talk in set complimentary phrases, and to honour by deep bows and genuflections. And if it were possible to enforce such a system on the entire population of a country, no doubt Confucius's definition of good government would be realized, and the Prince would be Prince, the Minister would be Minister, the father would be father, and the son would be son; universal humility would prevail, there would be no excess, no usurpation, and no irreverence.

But here again he over-estimated the force of example, and ignored the fact that in every country there is a lawless element which refuses to be kept in bounds by any but the firm hand of the law. Only once does he appear to have recognized this fact, and that is in his Commentary on the Yih king, where he says: "The superior man enjoys security, but he does not dispense with caution; he preserves what he possesses, yet does not forget that he may lose it, he rules in peace, but does not forget that rebellion is possible; then it is that personal tranquillity may be enjoyed, and the subjects of a state be protected."[1]

[1] Yih king. He tsze.

It is by the rules of propriety that the character is established, said Confucius, but it is from music that the finish is received. Thus music played in his system an important part in the government of a state. It produced a distinct impression on the people for good or for evil. So obvious was this impression to the eyes of wisdom, that we are told that when on his way to Ts'e, Confucius recognized in the gait and manners of a boy whom he met carrying a pitcher, the influence of the Shaou music, and told the driver of his carriage to hurry on to the capital. In another passage it is related that the sound of stringed instruments and singing at a place called Woo-shing caused him great delight, as he discerned by its tenour the effect produced on a people turbulent by nature by the wise and beneficent rule of his disciple Tsze-yew.[1] But music, like every other accomplishment, must be the outcome of sincerity. Without sincerity it is nothing worth. Bells and drums no more make up what is meant by music, than do gems and silks constitute propriety.[2] "If a man," said Confucius, " be without the virtues proper to humanity, what has he to do with either the rites of propriety or with music ? "[3]

But the great work which the Sage has to accomplish, and which is the object of his being, is to make the whole Empire peaceful and happy. This condition is arrived at when " the sovereign, by behaving to the aged as the aged should be behaved to, makes the people filial ; when by behaving to his elders as

[1] Lun yu, xvii. 4.　　[2] Ibid. xvii. 11.　　[3] Ibid. iii. 3.

elders should be behaved to, he teaches the people
brotherly submission ; and when, by treating com-
passionately the young and helpless, the people learn
to do the same."[1] Such was the state of things which
existed under the ideal rule of Yaou and Shun.
Appointed by the wish of Shang-te, in succession, to
the throne, and being gifted by heaven with perfect
natures, they followed without effort the heavenly
way, thus drawing down on themselves and their
fellow-men the blessings of Shang-te and the favour
of heaven.

[1] Ta heŏ, x. 1.

CHAPTER VI.

INCIDENTAL TEACHINGS OF CONFUCIUS.

SUCH are the main features of the teachings of Confucius. The welfare of the people, the right government of the state, and the prosperity of the empire, were the principal objects of his solicitude. But incidentally he touched on many subjects which only indirectly bear on these. His frequent themes of discourse were the " Book of Poetry,' "The Book of History," and the maintenance of the rules of propriety. He taught also letters, ethics, devotion of soul, and truthfulness. But extraordinary things, feats of strength, states of disorder, and spiritual beings, he did not like to talk about.[1]

As a moralist he must always rank high among the teachers of mankind. Five hundred years before Christ he taught—in the negative form, it is true,—that "most unshaken rule of morality, and foundation of all social virtue," "All things whatsoever ye would that men should do unto you do ye even so to them." "What you do not," he said, "want done to yourself do not do to others." [2] Logically it is obvious that

---

[1] Lun yu, vii. 17, 24, 20.   [2] Lun yu, xv. 23.

there is no difference between this and the Christian rule, and it is a notable fact that Confucius should have enunciated it. Like all that he taught, this maxim had its origin in the earlier classics, where in the matter of loyalty and filial piety men were told that they must not expect a display of those virtues towards themselves unless they in their turn practised them towards those to whom they were due. Reciprocity in practice was thus laid down as a rule of life, though it was left for Confucius to give expression to it in the abstract form.

Beyond this he did not go. Reciprocity, and that alone, was to be the guide of men's conduct to one another. "What do you say," said a disciple, "concerning the principle that injury should be recompensed with kindness?" The master said: "With what then will you recompense kindness? Recompense injury with justice, and recompense kindness with kindness." [1]

There is no spirit of forgiveness here, it is the stern law of an eye for an eye and a tooth for a tooth. Of the man who returns good for evil he speaks with contempt, as a cowardly creature who is "careful of his person." Far from checking the spirit of revenge, he inculcates it as a duty under certain circumstances. "'What course is to be pursued,' asked Tsze-hea, 'in the case of the murder of a father or a mother?' 'The son,' said the Sage, 'must sleep upon a mattress of grass, with his shield for his pillow; he must decline to take office; he must not live under the

[1] Lun yu, xiv. 36.

same heaven with his slayer.   When he meets him in the market-place, or the court, he must have his weapon ready to strike him.'   'And what should be done to avenge the murder of a brother?'   'The surviving brother must not take office in the same state with the slayer; yet if he go on his prince's service to the state where the slayer is, though he meet him he must not fight with him.'   'And what is to be done in the case of the murder of an uncle or a cousin?' 'In such a case the nephew or cousin is not the prin cipal.   If the principal on whom the revenge devolves can take it, he has only to stand behind with his weapon in his hands to support him.' "[1]

We are accustomed to such laws in the Old Testa ment history, and the condition of society in China at the time of Confucius was not much more advanced in such matters than that existing at the time of Moses.   And, indeed, the code of Confucius compares favourably with that promulgated by the Hebrew lawgiver.   Only on the slayer of a father or brother was vengeance to follow inevitably; whereas by the law of Moses no such restriction was laid on an avenger of blood.   This is all the more in Confucius's favour, since it is his unbounded reverence for the duty of filial piety which alone makes him call aloud for vengeance in the case of parricides.

The prominence given to filial piety by Confucius was, however, carried to lengths which blinded him to the difference between right and wrong.   He would have a father conceal the dishonesty of a son, and a son

---

[1] Legge's "Chinese Classics."

that of his father. "Uprightness is to be found in this,"[1] he said. This undue exaltation of one virtue to the detriment of others arose rather from a moral blindness than from any tendency towards deceit, for no one could be more constant in their exhortation to sincerity and honesty than Confucius. But just as a man shuts off from his view surrounding objects by holding some one thing close to his eyes, so Confucius lost all sense of the presence of other obligations by directing his attention too exclusively to the duty of filial piety. "Sincerity," said he, "is the end and beginning of things; without it there would be nothing."

Every student of Confucius must hold his personal character in high estimation. The narrative of few men's lives would be found so free from the taint of vice, and so full of many and estimable traits. Charges have been brought against him of want of truthfulness, but if we examine them they dwindle down to the mere question of what is truth. The main case against him is that when he was surrounded by the men of P'oo he regained his liberty by taking an oath that he would not proceed to the state of Wei, and as soon as his captors left him he continued his journey to that state. His defence of his conduct was that the oath had been extorted by force, and was not therefore binding. This is a nice question for casuists, but it is one upon which we do not intend to enter, being convinced that by most people he will not be held to be very blameworthy for that which, at the worst, was a mistaken notion of truthfulness.

---

[1] Lun yu. xiii. 18

A striking characteristic of Confucius was his humility; he scrupulously disclaimed all originality of doctrine. "A transmitter and not a maker, believing in and loving the ancients, I venture to compare myself with our old P'ang," was his description of himself. Nowhere did he depart from the language here used, and he resisted every temptation to usurp honours which did not belong to him. Though more deeply versed in the literature of his country than any of his contemporaries, he yet professed himself deficient in knowledge, though deeply enamoured of learning. Though looked upon by his fellow-men as a sage, he disclaimed the possession of the qualities of even a "superior man." "I am not virtuous enough," he said, "to be free from anxieties; not wise enough to be free from perplexities; and not bold enough to be free from fear."[1] In his duties as an official, as a son, and as a worshipper of the dead, he counted himself unworthy; and though at times the favoured counsellor of kings, he never strove to advance himself beyond his proper position, nor to make use of his influence to magnify himself in the eyes of his fellow men.

As he himself said, he sought an all-pervading unity in which the relations of life should be all strictly maintained, in which honour should be paid to those to whom it was due, and in which the stirrings of pleasure, anger, sorrow, or joy should be kept within their proper limits. Self was to be subdued, and the indulgence of the appetites was to be kept under con-

---

[1] Lun yu, xiv. 30.

trol. Gravity, generosity, sincerity, earnestness, and kindness were to be cultivated, and to the more sterling qualities of the mind should be added the attraction of accomplishments. For "when the solid qualities are in excess of accomplishments, we have rusticity, and when the accomplishments are in excess of the solid qualities we have the manners of a clerk. It is only when the two are equally blended that we have a man of complete virtue."[1] Of the importance of having a well-balanced character, which should display itself in a self-controlled manner, he spoke more than once. "Respectfulness," he said, "uninfluenced by the rules of propriety, becomes laborious bustle ; carefulness uninfluenced by the rules of propriety becomes timidity ; boldness uninfluenced by the rules of propriety becomes insubordination ; and straightforwardness uninfluenced by the rules of propriety becomes rudeness."[2] The accounts we have of his conduct both at home and abroad show how completely he carried into practice the rules he thus enunciated. Whether at court or in his own house he scrupulously avoided any breach of the strict observances, whether with regard to dress, food, or movements of the body, laid down by the ancients.

Poverty was his lot in life, and he never repined at the absence of wealth. "With coarse rice to eat," he said, "with water to drink, and my bended arm for my pillow, I am still contented and happy. Riches and honour acquired by wrong are to me as

---

[1] Lun yu, vi. 16.　　　　[2] Ibid. viii. 2.

floating clouds."[1]   But it was only in unusual cases of emergency that he was reduced to such hard fare as this.   On ordinary occasions, we are told, he was particular as to the wholesome quality of his food, and as to the way in which it was dressed ; he was careful in his choice of wine, and laid down for himself no limit in its use.   In all he did he showed himself to be a sincere admirer of the ancients, and in all he taught he was actuated by a sincere love for his fellow men.   He had very clearly in his mind a vision of a perfect state of society, and to this he strove to raise men's desires and capabilities.   The means he adopted to this end have been proved to be hopelessly inadequate, but his admirers can boast that he established a standard of morality which has helped to elevate his countrymen above all the other peoples of Asia, and to preserve the empire intact in all the vicissitudes of internal discords and foreign wars through which it has passed during four-and-twenty centuries.

Nothing has done more to maintain the existing order of things than the old doctrine he enforced that sovereigns were placed on the throne by heaven, and that their right to the sceptre lasted only as long as they walked in the heavenly path, and obeyed the heavenly decrees.   The departure from virtue was the signal for their condemnation, and absolved their subjects from the duty of obedience.   He thus implied the right, which Mencius openly claimed, of rebellion against impious rulers.   Nor has this right

Lun yu, vii. 15.

been allowed to remain a dead letter. Upwards of thirty times have there been changes of dynasty since the days of Confucius, and on each occasion the revolution has been justified by references to the teachings of the Sage and his great follower Mencius.

This separation of the office from the individual has rendered all dynastic loyalty impossible, and the people have seen line after line overthrown and their places occupied by strangers, and sometimes foreigners, with perfect equanimity. It is this which has made revolutions in China so comparatively peaceful. In a great majority of cases the provincial officials appointed by the fallen sovereign have been allowed to retain their posts under his successful rival. To them the emperor is the son of Heaven, whether he sits on the throne as the heir of a long line of emperors, or leaves his carpenter's bench, like the founder of the Ming dynasty, to overturn by the decree of Heaven the unworthy representative of Yaou and Shun. Still further, the Emperor destroys his individuality by dropping his name, and by taking instead of it a designation for his reign consisting of two carefully-selected characters of fortunate import. But as these have, until the advent to power of the present Manchoo dynasty, not unfrequently been changed during the reign of the same sovereign, few associations cling round any of them, and the adoption of a new title by a successful rebel destroys no cherished traditions, and uproots no personal memories.

Politically speaking, this is a strong point in the Confucian system, and as there is no *de jure* apart from the *de facto* royal house of China, it is a doctrine which has found ready acceptance by each and every successive sovereign, whose claim to the throne necessarily rests only on the will of Heaven as interpreted by the will of the people.

We have seen in what troublous times Confucius's lot was cast. They were days when warriors occupied the stage, and when men of letters were driven behind the scenes. Of current literature there was none beyond that which existed in the songs of the people, and the works of an earlier date were well nigh forgotten amid the clash of arms and struggles of contending chieftains. To compile and edit these, and to supplement them when it was necessary, was the work undertaken by Confucius, who thus brought again to light and made accessible to his countrymen the whole of the classical literature of the China of his day. Hence Confucius came to be regarded as the founder of learning, and when his works were recovered after the burning of the books by Che Hwang-te (circa 220 B.C.), the fame of all previous writers was merged in his who had preserved the glorious records of the golden age in Chinese history.

The revival of a literature which was looked upon as complete was hailed with delight by scholars, to whom the period since the savage decree of Che Hwang-te had been a night of mental darkness, and gained from them, by this circumstance, an exaggerated mead of praise. As some of the works were recovered piece-meal, some even by oral tradition, the study of the texts became a devouring pursuit among the literati. Commentaries and critical exegeses began speedily to appear, and instead of pursuing independent researches and bringing into play their powers of invention, the scholars of the day exhausted their ingenuity in elaborate treatises on minute verbal points of inquiry. The admiration thus bestowed on the works of Confucius and his disciples, with which were included the works of Mencius, gave rise to their being accepted as the only canonical works in the national literature, and as thus they received the titles of the "Five Classics" and the "Four Books." In the first category were placed the older works which were either wholly or in part compiled by Confucius, viz., the *Yih King,* or "Book of Changes"; the *She King,* or "Book of Poetry"; the *Shoo King,* or "Book of History"; the *Le Ke,* or "Book of Rites"; and the one work of which he was the author, the *Ch'un ts'ew,* or "Spring and Autumn Annals." The "Four Books" consisted of the *Ta heŏ,* or "Great Learning"; the *Chung yung,* or the "Doctrine of the Mean"; the *Lun yu,* or the "Confucian Analects"; and the *Măng tsze,* or "The Works of Mencius."

Having nothing whatever wherewith to compare these works, the contents of which were in complete harmony with the national mind, the people learnt to esteem them as the exponents of supreme wisdom. In every school they were adopted as text-books, and formed the only course of study pursued by every scholar throughout the empire. As soon as the system of competitive examination was introduced (631 A.D.) they were constituted the sole subjects for examination, and during all the centuries which have succeeded that period the same practice has been maintained. Thus for upwards of twelve hundred years the nine Confucian classics have been the main study of every generation of Chinamen from their childhood to their grave.

The effect of this complete absorption of the Confucian system into the national character has been to maintain the influence of the Sage as powerfully, or even more powerfully, than ever. Buddhism and Taouism have found their adherents almost entirely among the uneducated classes, and even these reject all doctrines which are inconsistent with the teachings of Confucius. No educated man would admit for a moment that he was a follower of either religion. To all such Confucius is guide, philosopher, and friend, and though fully recognised by them as a man, is worshipped as a god.

CHAPTER VII.

MENCIUS.

AFTER the death of Confucius the state of the empire grew worse and worse. The undutiful became more undutiful still, and the unruly more violent. The antagonism between the various states became even more pronounced, and the smaller principalities were being gradually swallowed up by their more powerful neighbours. To add still further to the perplexity of the time, men arose who preached new and strange doctrines, upsetting the recognised principles of right and wrong. Already men's minds felt the influence of the tone of thought in India which had given rise to Buddhism. Laou-tsze had taught the vanity of over-striving after earthly objects, and had held out the promise of a return to the Absolute to those who cultivated self-emptiness and humility. Some of his followers perverting his views had even proclaimed the possibility of the apotheosis of man, and the certainty of his acquiring magical powers by the exercise of sustained contemplation. All the old mental and moral landmarks had been overthrown, and the country was seething in agitation and confusion.

Such was the condition of the Empire when in the year 371 B.C. Mencius, on whom the mantle of Confucius was destined to fall, was born in the principality of Tsow. On arriving at man's estate he adopted, like his great prototype, the calling of a teacher, and gradually surrounded himself with a body of faithful and admiring disciples whom he educated to assist him in the work of perpetuating the doctrines of the Sage. He had no system of his own to enunciate, but clothing himself in the armour prepared for him by his master he went forth to combat the evils of the day, and just in proportion as these were greater and more complex than in the time of Confucius so was he bolder in attack and more subtle in argument than he. Where Confucius had chastised with whips he chastised with scorpions, and this not only when he was dealing with his equals or inferiors, but also where princes and governors were the objects of his wrath.

"May a subject put a ruler to death?" asked King Seuen of him. "He who outrages benevolence," answered Mencius, "is called a ruffian; and he who outrages righteousness is called a villain. The ruffian and villain we call a mere fellow. I have heard of the cutting off of the fellow Show [the last Emperor of the Shang Dynasty]; but I have not heard of a ruler having been put to death." The rights of the people were always uppermost in his thoughts. "The people," said he, "are the most important element in the country. . . . and the ruler is the lightest." The welfare of the people therefore should be the great concern of sovereigns, and he denounced with no faltering tongue the conduct of kings who by engaging in needless wars bring ruin and misery on

their subjects.   In all his utterances there was a fresh-
ness and vigour which are not to be found to the same
extent in the works of any other Chinese writer.   He
had a straightforward and incisive way of going to the
root of every matter.   Whether he had to contend
with visionaries such as Yang Choo and Mih Teih—
the first of whom preached the doctrine of "Each
one for himself" and the last that of "Universal
Love,"—or with unrighteous sovereigns such as King
Hwuy of Leang, or with argumentative disciples such
as Kaou-tsze, he at once struck at the source from
which their errors sprang.   He thrust on one side
all the false issues they raised or the excuses they
offered, and put his finger straight on the faulty argument, or the guilty motive, which invalidated their
theories or vitiated their conduct.   As he said himself,
"I understand words. . . . When speeches are one-
sided I know how the mind of the speaker is clouded
over; when they are extravagant I know wherein the
mind is snared; when they are all depraved, I know
how the mind has departed from principle; when
they are evasive, I know how the mind is at its wit's
end."

Like Confucius, Mencius earnestly longed to find
some ruler who would follow his counsels, and also
like Confucius, though he visited several courts and
was hospitably entertained, he failed in his great
object.   But though fortune refused to smile upon
him he found consolation in his retirement in the
belief that his want of success was the appointment of
Heaven.   "Heaven does not wish that the Empire
should enjoy tranquillity and good order," he said;

and it was therefore in no discontented spirit that he finally resigned all hope of seeing his principles carried into practice and devoted the fifteen years of life which remained to him to the compilation of his works and the instruction of his disciples.

Mencius was not formed of the stuff that courtiers are made of. During his lifetime his personal character was sufficient to save him from the consequences which might have been expected to follow from some of the views he expressed in conversations with the rulers of the states. But after his death, when his words only remained, and when his disinterested patriotism and commanding independence were forgotten, his merits received but scanty recognition at the hands of succeeding sovereigns. With the revival of learning under the Han Dynasty the attention of scholars was attracted to his writings, but it was not until the reign of Shin-tsung (A.D. 1068-1085), of the Sung Dynasty, that they were included among the Confucian classics, since which time, however, he has held a place, second only to that of Confucius, in the esteem of his countrymen.

CHAPTER VIII.

MODERN CONFUCIANISM.

WE have seen that Confucius's sun set under a cloud. The sovereigns of his day refused to listen to his instructions, and his were not doctrines to make their way unaided amongst the people. His system appealed, in the first instance, to the governing class, and had nothing in it to satisfy the spiritual wants of man. It was purely a politico-moral system, which needed patronage from above to enable it to gain currency in the empire. The condition of the country at the time of Confucius, and the strong opinions he held regarding the loyalty due to the falling house of Chow, deprived it of that patronage during his lifetime. But no sooner was he dead, than the Duke Gae, who had always respected him, but who had never submitted himself to his guidance, broke out in lamentations over him. "Heaven," said he, "has taken from me the aged man. There is no one now to assist me on the throne. Woe is me! Alas! O venerable Ne!" There is no reason to suppose that these regrets were insincere. The duke had constantly held long discussions with Confucius on the subject of government, and had no doubt profited by the advice given him. That he considered the adoption of Confucius's system in its entirety as impracticable as affairs then stood is plain, but he might well have been convinced of the practical wisdom of much that he taught.

The influence exercised by the disciples of the Sage was, however, no doubt considerable. Their. devotion to his memory and admiration for his doctrine, enforced as these were by Mencius, gained a certain amount of currency for the general outlines of his system, even in the unsettled state of society then existing; and when, after the struggles of the contending states had ended in the triumph of Ts'in, Che Hwng-te ordered all books to be burnt, the writings of Confucius were particularly pointed out for destruction. But they survived the *auto-da-fé*, and were preserved by ardent scholars in the walls of houses and beneath the ground, and in the memories of faithful disciples.

With the accession of the Han Dynasty (206 B.C.), a new era opened on the Confucian literature. Every encouragement was given by the Emperor Kaou Te to learning in all its branches, and to the study of the works of Confucius in particular. Penetrated with a sense of the value of the wisdom these contained, the emperor visited the tomb of the Sage in Loo, and there offered a bullock as a sacrifice in his honour. His successor, Ping Te (A.D. 1), conferred upon him the posthumous. title of "The Complete and Illustrious Duke Ne." Under this designation he was. known until Ho Te, of the Eastern Han Dynasty (A.D. 89), entitled him "The Illustrious and Honourable Earl." But it was not until nearly four hundred years after that he was canonized as "The Accomplished Sage." Subsequently frequent alterations were made by imperial order in this title, and in the reign of the Emperor Yuen-tsung, of the Tang Dynasty (715—742), he was dignified with the appellation of " Accomplished and Perspicacious King." The royal rank thus conferred upon him was the apology for moving his image in the Imperial College from the side of the hall where it had previously stood, to the centre facing the south, the true regal position. Desiring probably to show how much more intense was his admiration for the Sage than that which had animated any of his predecessors, Shin-tsung, of the Sung Dynasty (1068—1086), advanced him to imperial rank, and styled him " Emperor." Later again, Ching-tsung, of the Yuen Dynasty (1295—1308), conferred upon him the designation of " Most Complete and Perfect Sage, the Accomplished and Perspicacious King"; and the title which he now bears of " The Perfect Sage, the Ancient Teacher Confucius," was designed by the Emperor She-tsung, of the Ming Dynasty (1506—1522).

The emperors of the present dynasty have wisely abstained from adding any new titles of honour to the memory of the Sage. Their unfeigned zeal in the cause of his doctrines has been rightly considered by them to be more truly laudatory than the mere addition or change of a character in his posthumous honours. " The Throneless King " is, however, an apt designation, which is common among the people, for one who has exercised such supreme dominion over the minds of his countrymen for so many centuries.

But the titles conferred on Confucius by the emperors of China were not mere words. From the time of the Emperor Kaou Te (206—194 B.C.) to the present day, Confucius has been, outwardly at least, the object of the most supreme veneration and devout worship of every occupant of the throne. Temples have been erected to his honour in every city in the empire, and his worship, which was originally confined to his native state, has for the last twelve hundred years been as universal as the study of the literature which goes by his name.

The most important and sacred temple is that adjoining his tomb in Shantung, on which all the art of Chinese architecture has been lavished. The main building consists of two stories, the upper verandah surrounding which "rests on gorgeous marble pillars, twenty-two feet high, and about two feet in diameter, which at a distance appear as if huge dragons were coiled around them and hanging from the top. . . . The tiles of the roof are of yellow porcelain, as in Peking, and the ornamentation of the eaves is covered with wire-work to keep it from the birds. Inside the building is the image or statue of Confucius, in a gorgeously-curtained shrine, holding in his hand a slip of bamboo, such as was used for writing upon in his days. The statue is about eighteen feet by six feet, and is life-like. Confucius was tall, strong, and well-built, with a full red face, and large and heavy head. . . . On the tablet is the simple inscription—'The most Holy prescient Sage Confucius—His Spirit's resting-place.' On the east side are images of his favourite disciples,

M

arranged according to the estimation in which he is said to have held them. . . . The roof of the building is crowded with tablets, hung up in honour of the Sage, each vying with another in extravagant praise. . . . Before him, and also before his disciples, were the usual frames for sacrifices, and in front of these, beautiful incense-pots; beside them were several most interesting relics, such as vases, said to be of the Shang Dynasty, B.C. 1610, the work of which was superb. There were also two bronze elephants, reported to be of the Chow Dynasty, and a table of that same era of dark red wood.

" On the west side are two temples; one in front, in honour of the father of Confucius . . . and one behind, in honour of his mother. . . . On the east side are temples to his five ancestors, and a large block of marble, whereon is a genealogical tree, giving all the branches of his family. . . The building behind the grand temple is the temple in honour of his wife, in which was only a tablet and no image. The second temple behind that contained four tablets, erected by K'ang-he in his honour, one character on each, and the interpretation was, 'The perspicuous teacher of ten thousand kingdoms.' Here also are three pictures of the Sage on marble; one an old man, full-length, rather dim, having no date; the second smaller, with seal characters on the side; the third, and best, giving only his head and shoulders. These varied somewhat, but were substantially alike. All of them have the mouth or lips open and front teeth exposed, and the full, contemplative eyes. Immediately behind these are gravings on marble, illustrating all the chief incidents of his life, with appropriate explanations at the side. Of these there were altogether one hundred and twenty slabs, which are built into the wall."[1]

Second only to this temple is the Kwo-tsze-keen, at Peking, the main difference between the two being that at the Kwo-tsze-keen there are no images ; but, on the other hand, it contains evidence of the political homage paid to Confucius in the shape of six monuments with yellow tiled roofs, recording the following foreign conquests of the Emperors K'ang-he, Yung-ching, and K'een-lung :—

1704. K'ang-he, conquest of Shomo, Western Mongolia.

1726. Yung-ching, conquest of Tsing-hai, or Eastern Tibet.

1750. K'een-lung, conquest of Kwei-chow.

1760. K'een-lung, conquest of Dsungaria.

1760. K'een-lung, conquest of Kashagaria.

1777. K'een-lung, conquest of the Meaou country in Sze-chuen.

To this temple the emperor goes in state twice a year, and having twice knelt, and six times bowed his head to the earth, invokes the presence of the Sage in these words : " Great art thou, O perfect Sage ! Thy virtue is full ; thy doctrine is complete. Among mortal men there has not been thine equal. All kings honour thee. Thy statutes and laws have come gloriously down. Thou art the pattern of this Imperial school. Reverently have the sacrificial vessels

[1] "Journies in North China." By Rev. A. Williamson.

been set out. Full of awe, we sound our drums and bells."[1] The spirit being now supposed to be present, the ceremony is gone through of presenting the appropriate offerings, which consist, according to circumstances, of pieces of satin, wine, salted tiger's flesh, dried fish, dried and minced venison, minced hare, minced fish, a pure black bullock, a sheep or a pig.

The officiating mandarin then reads the following prayer:—"On this . . . month of this . . . year, I A.B., the Emperor, offer a sacrifice to the philosopher K'ung, the ancient Teacher, the perfect Sage, and say,—O Teacher, in virtue equal to heaven and earth, whose doctrines embrace the past times and the present, thou didst digest and transmit the six classics, and didst hand down lessons for all generations! Now in this second month of spring (or autumn), in reverent observance of the old statutes, with victims, silks, spirits, and fruits, I carefully offer sacrifice to thee. With thee are associated the philosopher Yen, continuator of thee; the philosopher Tsăng, exhibitor of thy fundamental principles; the philosopher Tsze-sze, transmitter of thee; and the philosopher Măng (Mencius), second to thee. May thou enjoy the offerings."[2]

As will be inferred from this prayer, the image of Confucius does not stand alone, but is surrounded by images of his principal disciples, while in a hall at the back of that dedicated to him are ranged those of his ancestors. Occasionally different emperors have

---

[1] Legge's Prolegomena to the Confucian Analects.   [2] Ibid.

visited his tomb in Shan-tung, at which times the imperial pilgrims have worshipped with extraordinary solemnity at his shrine in the adjoining temple. K'ang-he, the most celebrated both as a ruler and a scholar of the emperors of the present dynasty, went on such a pilgrimage, and "set the example of kneeling thrice, and each time laying his forehead thrice in the dust, before the image of the Sage."[1]

In the provinces 1,500 temples are dedicated to his worship, where on the first and fifteenth day of each month sacrificial services are performed before his image, and once in the spring and autumn the local officials go in state to take part in acts of specially solemn worship. According to the *Shing meaou che*, or "History of the Temples of the Sage," as many as 6 bullocks, 27,000 pigs, 5,800 sheep, 2,800 deer, and 2,700 hares are sacrificed on these occasions, and at the same time 27,600 pieces of silk are offered on his shrine.

Flowing naturally from this worship of Confucius comes the profound respect and reverence which are shown to every work of which he was the author, or which appeared with his *imprimatur*. In the great quadrangle in the Kwo-tsze-keen at Peking are ranged in long arcades rows of stone slabs, on which are engraved the texts of the classics, while "in the centre stands one of the most striking specimens of Chinese architecture, consisting in a lofty pavilion-shaped building, erected upon a platform of white marble placed in the midst of a circular piece of water, itself walled in with marble, and across which access is

[1] Legge's Prolegomena to the Analects.

given to the building by four marble arches at the cardinal points. In this building, which represents the *Pi yung*, or Imperial College of Antiquity, each sovereign is held bound to enthrone himself once in the course of his reign, to preside over a solemn assemblage of all the scholars of the capital, in whose hearing a classical essay, nominally composed by his majesty, and hence designated *Yu lun*, is recited." [1]

In the constant chorus of admiration which has been outpoured on the memory of Confucius by every generation of scholars since his day there has been scarcely a discordant note. His doctrine of the natural goodness of man's nature has been contested, and various interpretations have been placed upon his leading doctrines, some commentators describing them as the utterances of a god, and others as those of a plain matter-of-fact man who was anxious to do all the good which lay within his power. The writer of the greatest eminence who has had the boldness openly to attack him was Wang Ch'ung (19—90 A.D.), who, in a work in thirty books, entitled *Lun·hăng*, or critical Disquisitions, "handles mental and physical problems in a style and with a boldness unparalleled in Chinese literature," and devotes a chapter to exposing the exaggerations and contradictions of which he considered Confucius to have been guilty.

The doctrines Confucius enunciated were so plainly contradicted by events within his own experience, that it is difficult to understand how they can have been sustained by Confucianists of later ages. The explanation of the difficulty probably is that the sayings of the Sage have been formulated by his disciples into

[1] Mayers's " Chinese Government."

a system of which he was entirely innocent, for a careful study of the sayings of Confucius tends to show that he did not devise any regular system, either of ethics or of politics, in his own mind, but simply gave utterance as occasion arose to disjointed maxims, many of which have been misunderstood, and most of which are mere quotations from the earlier classics.

Still there remains a substantial substratum of wisdom in his teachings, and this it is which forms the *raison d'être* of Confucianism.   There is much that has sunk to the bottom, but there is much that still floats.   Few at the present day would agree with Confucius in his estimate of the extraordinary influence which is to be exercised by any single man who is either born a sage or has become a "superior man" by self-cultivation, and few again would entirely hold with him in his views on the nature of man, and on the efficacy of the means which he would employ to perfect it.   But at the same time his maxims of general morality are such as will command respect through all time, and carry as much weight now in China as they did when the revival of learning first gave birth to the profound admiration of his works which characterized the opening of the earlier Han Dynasty.

Towards the close of the seventeenth century the Emperor K'ang-he, whose admiration for Confucius has been exemplified above, issued sixteen maxims, founded on the teachings of the Sage, for the guidance of the people, whose morality "had for some time been daily declining, and whose hearts were not as of old." He thus summed up, as it were, all the essential points in the Confucian doctrine, and thus he wrote:—

1. "Esteem most highly filial piety and brotherly submission, in order to give due prominence to the social relations."

2. "Behave with generosity to the branches of your kindred, in order to illustrate harmony and benignity."

3. "Cultivate peace and concord in your neighbourhoods, in order to prevent quarrels and litigations."

4. "Recognise the importance of husbandry and the culture of the mulberry-tree, in order to ensure a sufficiency of clothing and food."

5. "Show that you prize moderation and economy, in order to prevent the lavish waste of your means."

6. "Make much of the colleges and seminaries, in order to make correct the practice of the scholars."

7. "Discountenance and banish strange doctrines, in order to exalt the correct doctrine."

8. "Describe and explain the laws, in order to warn the ignorant and obstinate."

9. "Exhibit clearly propriety and yielding courtesy, in order to make manners and customs good."

10. "Labour diligently at your proper callings, in order to give settlement to the aims of the people."

11. "Instruct sons and younger brothers, in order to prevent them from doing what is wrong."

12. "Put a stop to false accusations, in order to protect the honest and the good."

13. " Warn against sheltering deserters, in order to avoid being involved in their punishments."

14. " Promptly and fully pay your taxes, in order to avoid the urgent requisition of your quota."

15. " Combine in hundreds and tithings, in order to put an end to thefts and robbery."

16. " Study to remove resentments and angry feelings, in order to show the importance due to the person and life." [1]

But it will naturally be asked, Wherein lay the secret of the vast influence which has been exercised by Confucius? And to this we answer, first, that being a Chinaman of Chinamen, his teachings were specially suited to the nature of those he taught. The Mongolian mind being eminently phlegmatic and unspeculative, naturally rebels against the idea of investigating matters which are beyond its experiences, and its calm, placid habit forbids its being the instigator of fiery tempers and hot-headed crimes. With the idea, therefore, of a future life still unawakened, a plain, matter-of-fact system of morality, such as that enunciated by Confucius, was sufficient for all the wants of the Chinese. Secondly, it was to the interest of both the rulers and the ruled to support his doctrines. The *de facto* ruler found in him a tower of strength ; for if the throne was the reward vouchsafed by Heaven for eminent virtue, then he who occupied it in peace must necessarily have an unassailable right to it; and the constant exhortations to loyalty to be found on every page of the Confucian

---

[1] Legge's " Imperial Confucianism," lecture I.

writings cannot but have been grateful to the ears of sovereigns.

The ruled, on the other hand, felt that they were supreme in the estimation of the Sage. The promotion of their interests and material well-being was the first duty of the sovereign, and the extent of their loyalty was to be measured by his success in this direction. He recognised no ranks or titles but those won by merit, and thus every office in the State was open to every one alike. The people were to be well cared for, and in case of neglect or oppression they had the right of rebellion. The sovereign was the vice-regent of Heaven, but only as long as he walked in the heavenly way were the unswerving loyalty and devotion of his subjects due to him.

And thirdly, the possession of so highly-prized a literature at so early a date having suggested its adoption as the curriculum in schools and the test of scholarship at all examinations, the people, ignorant of all else, have learned to look upon it as containing the quintessence of wisdom, and its author as the wisest of mankind. It might be considered impossible to calculate the effects of the concentration of a nation's mind century after century on the study of any given text book; but in China we have the result worked out before us, and we find that it has amounted to the absolute subjection of upwards of forty generations of Chinamen to the dicta of one man.

TAOUISM.

TAOUISM,

CHAPTER I.

INTRODUCTORY.

In the condition of China under the Chow Dynasty we have traced the motives which drew Confucius from his study, and impelled him to grapple with the times. The disorder, lust, and violence which he saw rampant about him were so many irresistible goads to him to warn and exhort his countrymen and their rulers in season and out of season. His study of history had taught him how much may be done by one man. He had learnt that Yaou and Shun and Woo and Wăn had at different times restored the empire from a state of anarchy to a condition of peace and tranquillity by the force of their examples and the influence of their teachings, and believing himself to have a heaven-sent mission to repeat their reforms, he laboured day and night to impress on his hardened contemporaries the evils of their ways.

We have seen how completely unsuccessful he was in his crusade against the iniquities of the time, although it must be admitted that he had many of the qualities of a reformer. His moral character was beyond reproach, he had great persistency, his mental powers

were of a high order, and he was armed with arguments
as persuasive as any which then had or since have
had currency in China. Where he failed, therefore,
it was not likely that others would succeed. Many
tried, and most ended by acting in harmony with the
principle laid down by Confucius, that "a superior
man should not enter a tottering state," and retired
altogether from political life. Such men watched with
scorn Confucius's efforts. They saw him travelling
through the country from court to court attended by a
crowd of admiring disciples, and they saw him driven
by neglect to shake off from his feet the dust of capital
after capital. No wonder they imputed to him ambitious and unworthy motives. No wonder they
sneered at him, as did the recluse of whom he asked
his way to Ts'ai, and taunted him with his courtier-like
ways and proud airs.

Among these recluses arose one who was noted as
a deep and original thinker, and who became the
founder of Taouism. This was Laou-tsze, the old
philosopher, who was born about fifty years before
Confucius. Laou-tsze was therefore advanced in age
when his great contemporary rose to eminence, and
having long found out the hopelessness of attempting
to stem the evil current of the age, he looked on
with supercilious contempt at the futile efforts made
by Confucius in the same direction.

History, which has been so profuse in its details of
the life of Confucius, has been equally reticent on
the subject of Laou-tsze's career. We have minute
accounts of all that befell Confucius from his early
manhood to his grave. We are taken into his study

and his dining-room and even into his bed-chamber. His appearance is as familiar to us as that of Shakespeare, and we know how he behaved during thunderstorms and what he ate with his rice. None of these details could we spare. They all serve to set the man before us and to illustrate his character and that of his teachings. But in the case of Laou-tsze no such intimacy is allowed us. Even his parentage is surrounded with uncertainty, of his life we know nothing except one or two facts, and we are in ignorance of the manner of his death and of the place of his burial. And yet he was one of the deepest thinkers China has produced.

According to the great historian Sze-ma Tseen, Laou-tsze's surname was Le (a plum-tree), his name Urh (an ear), his style Pih-yang, and his posthumous title Tan, or flat-eared. His father is said to have been a peasant, who married at the age of seventy a woman little more than half his age. The similarity between this account and that given of the disparity between the ages of the father and mother of Confucius makes one hesitate to accept it. But whether true or false, he is said to have first seen the light in the year 604 B.C., at the village of Keŭh jin, or "Oppressed Benevolence," in the parish of Le, or "Cruelty," in the district of K'oo, or "Bitterness," in the state of T'soo, or "Suffering." By some the very existence of such a person as Laou-tsze has been doubted, and if he really were only a fiction of the imagination, no more appropriate names than these could have been chosen for the birthplace of a man of virtue, who was driven from office into solitude and oblivion by the cruelty and oppression of the time. But those who put full faith in his existence identify this city of Bitterness with the ancient K'oo, which stood near to the modern Kwei-tih Foo, in the east of the province of Honan. At K'oo-yang, a house in which Laou-tsze is said to have lived is shown, and at the same place his memory is still further preserved in a temple which is dedicated to his honour.

Sze-ma Tseen tells us nothing of his boyhood or of his early manhood, but merely mentions that he held office at the imperial court of Chow, as *Show tsang shih che she*, or " Keeper of the Archives." The title of this office has been variously translated. Julien and Pauthier give it as above, Dr. Legge translates it " Treasury-keeper," and Mr. Watters prefers " Keeper of the Imperial Museum." But apart from the fact that it was to Laou-tsze that Confucius went to gain information on the ancient rites and ceremonies of the state of Chow, which would naturally be sought for in the State archives, it is stated in the Koo kin t'oo shoo tseih ch'ing, that one object of Confucius's visit to the philosopher was to hand him a book to be placed in the archives. This last incident is possibly legendary, but it shows what the nature of his duties was understood to have been by his countrymen.

All authorities agree, however, that it was while Laou-tsze held this post at the court of Chow that, like another Aristotle, Confucius visited the Chinese Socrates. The fifty-one years through which Confucius had at this time passed had not been unaccompanied by many disappointments, and, according to

Chwang-tsze, he poured the tale of his experiences into the ears of the old philosopher, who rebuked his reforming zeal in these words: "If it be known that he who talks errs by excess in arguing, and that he who hears is confused by too much talk, the Way can never be forgotten."

On another occasion, when Confucius had been enlarging on his admiration for the ancients, the cynical recluse cut him short by saying, "The men of whom you speak, sir, have, with their bones, already mouldered into dust, and only their words remain. Moreover, if the superior man gets his opportunity, he mounts his car and takes office; and if he does not get his opportunity, he goes through life like a wisp of straw rolling over sand. I have heard that a good merchant, who has his treasure-house well stored, appears devoid of resources, and that the superior man of perfect excellence has an outward semblance of stupidity. Put away, sir, your haughty airs and many desires, your flashy manner and extravagant will; these are all unprofitable to you. This is all I have to say to you."

From this interview Confucius retired discomfited, and said to his disciples, "I know how birds can fly, how fishes can swim, and how beasts can run. The runner, however, may be snared, the swimmer may be hooked, and the flyer may be shot with an arrow. But there is the dragon; I cannot tell how he mounts on the wind through the clouds, and rises to heaven. To-day I have seen Laou-tsze, and can only compare him to the dragon." The formalities and professions of virtue in which Confucius delighted to indulge, and

which were esteemed by Laou-tsze as so many proofs
of his being far from arriving at Taou, irritated the
philosophically-minded keeper of the archives, who
seems to have taken a pleasure in shocking and
mystifying his matter-of-fact visitor.

This last is the only interview between Confucius
and Laou-tsze recorded by Sze-ma Tseen ; and the
same historian tells us, that shortly after this, foreseeing
the inevitable downfall of the state of Chow,—a fact
to which Confucius was blind, Laou-tsze resigned his
office and went into retirement. It not unfrequently
happens that at times of disorganization and disruption
in temporal affairs, a co-ordination in spiritual matters
takes place. Men's minds being forcibly diverted from
the consideration of civil government, are driven to
the contemplation of immaterial concerns. Thus it
was with Laou-tsze : being relieved from the cares of
office, he " cultivated *Taou* and Virtue, and resigned
himself to a life of retirement and oblivion."

But before long so disorganized did the state of
society become, that his place of retreat ceased to
furnish him protection against violence, and he therefore took his journey into a far country, passing out
of the State which he had served so long by the Han-
koo Pass, in the prefecture of Chen Chow, in the
province of Honan. Here he devoted some time to
instructing Yin He, the keeper of the Pass, in the
doctrines of Taou. After which he went on his
journey westward, and from that moment all trace of
him has been lost.

We are told, however, that he left a son, named
Tsung, who became a general in the state of Wei, and

was rewarded for his services by a fief at Twan-kan. From Tsung five generations in direct descent are traced, the last of which settled in the state of T'se. From this point again history fails to follow the fortunes of the family: and thus is afforded another contrast with the family of Confucius, whose representative at the present day enjoys the title of Duke, and a liberal pension.

But though history contains but scanty references to the life of Laou-tsze, religious records, like the "Aurea Legenda" of Western Hagiology, abound with marvellous tales of his birth and career. By some writers he is declared to have been a spiritual being, and the embodiment of Taou; without beginning and without cause; the ancestor of the original breath; without light, form, sound, or voice; having neither ancestors nor descendants; dark, yet having within himself a spiritual substance; and that substance was truth. According to these authors, his appearance during the Chow dynasty was only one of his avatars. At the time of the three emperors, he first appeared as a man under the name of Yuen-chung-fa-sze, and the intervening period between this and his final birth as Laou-tsze witnessed no fewer than ten incarnations.

Equally bold legend-mongers aver that his mother conceived him in consequence of the emotion she felt at the sight of a falling star; that for eighty-one long years he remained concealed in the womb, and that at length he was born under the shade of a Le, or plum-tree. His appearance at his birth, which was that of an old man with grey hair, gained for him his

name of Laou-tsze, or Old Boy, by which he is still
known. With his first breath he was endowed with
complete intelligence, and possessed of the power of
speech. Pointing to the tree under which his mother
had a few minutes before given him birth, he said :
" Le [Plum] shall be my surname." Later writers
state that as soon as he was born he mounted in the
air, like Sâkyamuni, St. Francis of Assisi, Ignatius
Loyola, and other saints, and pointing with his left
hand to heaven and with his right hand to earth, he
said : " In heaven above and on earth beneath *Taou*
alone is worthy of honour." His complexion was
white and yellow ; his ears were of an extraordinary
size, and were each pierced with three passages. He
had handsome eyebrows, large eyes, ragged teeth, a
double-ridged nose, and a square mouth ; on each
foot he had ten toes, and each hand was ornamented
with ten lines.

Thus distinguished from the common herd of men,
it is not surprising that Yin He, the keeper of the
Han-koo kwan, on seeing him approach the pass,
should have at once recognised him as being no ordinary man. On the other hand, Laou-tsze, perceiving
that Yin He possessed the qualifications of a disciple,
willingly consented to abide with him for a while, to
instruct him in the principles of Taou. At last the
time came when the philosopher announced his departure westward. Yin He begged earnestly to be
allowed to accompany him, protesting that he was
willing to follow him through fire and water. But
Laou-tsze forbade him. " Then," said the disciple,
" I pray you, give a record of your philosophy."

Upon which Laou-tsze expounded to him his doctrines, and left him a work in five thousand characters on the subject of *Taou* (the Way) and *Tĭh* (Virtue).

But there was yet another obstacle to his departure to be overcome. The philosopher's servant, Seu keă, who had served him for two hundred years without receiving any wages, finding that his master was going to take a journey whither he knew not, suddenly demanded his arrears of pay, which upon calculation were found to amount to 72,000 ounces of silver. Fearing to face his master, he induced an acquaintance to ask Yin He to broach the subject to Laou-tsze. The acquaintance being ignorant of the relation existing between the master and servant, and already deeming in anticipation Seu keă to be a rich man, promised him his daughter in marriage. The beauty of the girl added to the persistency of the serving-man, whom Laou-tsze summoned to his presence. "I hired you originally," he said, "to perform the most humble duties; your circumstances were poor, and no one else would employ you. I have given you the talisman of long life, and it is due to this alone that you are now in existence. How have you so far forgotten the benefits I have heaped upon you as to cover me with reproaches? I am now about to set out for the Western Sea [the Caspian]; I intend to visit the kingdoms of Ta T'sin [the Roman empire], of Ke-pin [Cabul], of Teen-choo [India], and of Gan-se [Parthia]; and I order you to act as my charioteer thitherwards. On my return, I will pay you that which I owe you."

But Seu keă still refused to obey. Whereupon

Laou-tsze ordered him to lean forward and to open his mouth, and instantly there escaped from his lips the talisman, and at the same moment his body became a heap of dry bones.

At the earnest prayer of Yin He the ungrateful servant was restored to life, and was dismissed with a present of 20,000 ounces of silver. Having nothing further to detain him, Laou-tsze bade farewell to the keeper of the pass, and mounting upon a cloud, disappeared into space.

Some Taouist writers claim Laou-tsze as the author of nine hundred and thirty of the current works on the superstitious vanities of modern Taouism, and add complacently that all other books are unworthy of the same regard, having been secretly added by the followers of Taou in later ages.

As stated above, Sze-ma Tseen makes mention of only one interview between Confucius and Laou-tsze; but as the main object of the Sage's visit to Chow was to receive instruction from the Keeper of the Archives, it is more than probable that, as stated in the Kea yu, Le-ke, and elsewhere, their intercourse was frequent. On one occasion, Laou-tsze saw Confucius engaged in study, and asked what book he was reading. "The *Yih-king* [the Book of Changes]," replied Confucius; "the sages of antiquity used to read it also." "The sages were able to read it," answered Laou-tsze; "but you, to what end do you read it? What is the groundwork of the book?" "It treats of humanity and justice," answered the Sage.

"The justice and humanity of the day are no more

than empty names; they only serve as a mask to cruelty, and trouble the hearts of men; disorder was never more rife than at present. The pigeon does not bathe all day to make itself white; nor does the crow paint itself each morning to make itself black. The heaven is naturally elevated, the earth is naturally gross; the sun and the moon shine naturally; the stars and planets are naturally arranged in their places; the plants and trees fall naturally into classes, according to their species. So, sir, if you cultivate Taou, if you throw yourself towards it with all your soul, you will arrive at it. To what good is humanity and justice? You are like a man who beats a drum while searching for a truant sheep. Master, you only trouble man's nature."[1]

In this passage we have a clear exposition of the leading differences between Confucius and Laou-tsze. Confucius held that the chief requirement of the age was the rectification of names. He would have men practise humanity and call it humanity; he would have men dutiful to their parents, and call it filial piety; he would have men serve their sovereign with their whole heart, and call it loyalty. Laou-tsze, on the contrary, held that when-men professed to be humane, filial, and loyal, it was a sure sign that the substance had disappeared, and that the shadow only remained. The pigeon is not white on account of much bathing, nor does the crow paint itself black. If the pigeon began to bathe itself, and the crow to

[1] Julien, Introduction to "Le Livre de la Voie et de la Vertu."

paint itself, would it not be a sign that they had lost their original colours? And so with men. If all men were humane, filial, and loyal, no one would profess these virtues, and they would therefore never be named. And in the same way, if all men were virtuous, the names even of vices would be unknown.

No wonder that Confucius searched for twenty years for the Taou of Laou-tsze and found it not. " If Taou," said Laou-tsze, " could be offered to men, there is no one who would not wish to offer it to his prince; if it could be presented to men, there is no one who would not wish to present it to his parents ; if it could be announced to men, there is no one who would not wish to announce it to his brethren ; if it could be transmitted to men, there is no one who would not wish to transmit it to his children. Why then are not you able to acquire it? This is the reason : it is that you are incapable of giving it an asylum in the bottom of your heart."

To this Confucius could only reply, in the spirit of a Pharisee, by pleading his works of merit. " I have edited the Book of Odes," said he, " the Book of History, the Book of Rites, the Treatise on Music, and the Book of Transformations, and I have composed the Spring and Autumn Annals ; I have read the Maxims of the. Ancient Kings ; I have brought to light the splendid deeds of the Sages, and yet no one deigns to employ me. It is difficult, I see, to persuade men."

" The six liberal arts," replied Laou-tsze, " are an old heritage from the kings of antiquity. That with which you occupy yourself results only in obsolete examples, and all you do is to walk in the footprints of the past, without producing anything new."

From this interview Confucius returned to his disciples, and for three days did not utter a word. According to his own account, Laou-tsze exercised a complete fascination over him. He felt, when conversing with the older philosopher, that he was in the presence of a master mind, and the merciless criticism of which his doctrines were the object, shook his faith somewhat in their truth. "At his voice," said he, "my mouth gaped wide, my tongue protruded, and my soul was plunged in trouble."

To Yang-tsze, a disciple of Confucius, Laou-tsze spoke in the same strain. "The spots of the tiger and of the leopard, and the agility of the monkey, are that which exposes them to the arrows of the hunter." And in reply to a question concerning the administration of the illustrious kings of antiquity, he said, "Such was the administration of the illustrious kings, that their merits overspread the empire unknown to themselves; the influence of their example extended to all beings; they effected the happiness of the people without letting them feel their presence. Their virtue was so sublime that human speech is unable to express it; they lived in an impenetrable retreat, and were absorbed in Taou.

CHAPTER II.

THE TAOU TIH KING.

It has been stated above that on leaving China on his last impenetrable journey, Laou-tsze put into the hands of the Guardian of the Pass the results of his many years of lonely meditation in the shape of a book containing five thousand characters. Probably no widely-spread religion was ever founded on so small a base. Like an inverted pyramid, the ever-increasing growth of Taouist literature and superstitious doctrines which make up the sum of modern Taouism, rests on this small volume as its ultimate support. We say "ultimate" advisedly, for other works have long surpassed it in popularity. Its philosophical speculations are far beyond the reach of the ordinary reader, and even scholars are obliged to confess that they have but a general idea of the meaning of the old recluse. "It is not easy," says one of the best-known native commentators, "to explain clearly the more profound passages of Laou-tsze; all that science is able to do is to give the general sense." [1]

To European scholars the difficulty is even greater. As Rémusat remarks in his *Mémoire de Lao-tseu*, "The text is so full of obscurity, we have so few

[1] Julien, Introduction to "Le Livre de la Voie, et de la Vertu."

means of acquiring a perfect understanding of it, so
little knowledge of the circumstances to which the
author makes allusion ; we are, in a word, so distant
in all respects from the ideas under the influence of
which he wrote, that it would be temerity to pretend
to reproduce exactly the sense which he had in view,
when that sense is beyond our grasp." It is, however, always easy to affix a plausible interpretation to
that which is not susceptible of any definite explanation, and consequently a host of commentators and
translators have arisen, who find in the *Taou-tih-
king* confirmation of their preconceived theories of
his meaning, and of their preconceived wishes on
his behalf. The early Jesuit missionaries found in
its pages a prophetic knowledge of the truths of
Christianity. According to Montucci, " the principal
object of the *Taou-tih-king* is to establish a singular
knowledge of a Supreme Being in three persons.
Many passages speak so clearly of a triune God, that
to any one reading this book it will be plain that the
mystery of the Holy Trinity was revealed to the
Chinese more than five centuries before the coming
of Jesus Christ."

Amiot thought he recognised the Three Persons of
the Trinity in the first phrase of the fourteenth chapter
of the *Taou-tih-king*, which he translated thus: "That
which is as though it were visible, and yet cannot be
seen, is called *Khi* (to be read *I*); that which is
audible, and yet speaks not to the ears, is called *Hi ;*
that which is as though it were within one's reach,
and yet cannot be touched, is called *Wei.*" Rémusat
went even beyond Amiot, and recognised in the three

characters *I, Hi, Wei*, the word Jehovah. "These three characters," said he, "have no sense as employed here, they simply represent sounds foreign to the Chinese language, whether they are articulated as one word (IHV), or whether the initials I., H., V., are taken separately. . . . The trigrammatic name I-Hi-Wei, or IHV, being, as we have seen, foreign to the Chinese language, it is interesting to discover the origin. This word appears to me to be to all intents identical to that of Iaῶ (a variant of the Hebrew tetragramme יהוה, Jéhova), the name which, according to Diodore of Sicily, the Jews gave to God. It is very remarkable that the most exact transcription of this celebrated name is found in a Chinese book, for Laou-tsze has preserved the aspiration which the Greeks were not able to express with the letters of their alphabet. On the other side we find the Hebrew tetragramme reduced to three letters in the *Taou-tĭh-king*. This doubtless makes no difference in the pronunciation, for to all appearance the last ה of יהוה (Jéhova) is not pronounced. . . . The fact of a Hebrew or Syrian word in a Chinese book, a fact hitherto unknown, is certainly singular enough, and it remains, I think, completely proved, though there remains much to be done before it can be satisfactorily explained. . . . This name, so well preserved in the *Taou-tĭh-king* that it may be said that the Chinese had a better knowledge and a more exact transcript than the Greeks, is a particularity truly characteristic. It appears to me impossible to doubt that this name did not originate in this form in Syria, and I regard it as an incontestable proof of the route which the ideas which we call Pythagorian and Platonian have followed in reaching China."

But putting aside these fanciful speculations, we find that in the *Taou-tih king* Laou tsze has elaborated his idea of the relations existing between the Universe and that which he calls *Taou*. The primary meaning of this name of a thing which he declares to be "without name," is "The Way"; hence it has acquired the symbolical meanings of "the right course of conduct," "reason," and it also signifies "the Word" (Logos). By all these meanings it has been severally rendered by the translators of Laou-tsze's celebrated work. In support of each rendering it is possible to adduce quotations from the text, but none is the equivalent of Laou-tsze's *Taou*. The word *Taou* is not the invention of Laou-tsze. It was constantly in the mouth of Confucius, and with him it meant the "Way." The Buddhists also used it in the sense of "Intelligence," and called their co-religionists Taou-jin, or "Men of Intelligence." If we were compelled to adopt a single word to represent the *Taou* of Laou-tsze, we should prefer the sense in which it is used by Confucius, "the Way," that is, μέθοδος. "If I were endowed with prudence, I should walk in the great *Taou*. . . . The great *Taou* is exceedingly plain, but the people like the foot-paths," said Laou-tsze (chapter 53). But it is more than the way. It is the way and the way-goer. It is an eternal road; along it all beings and things walk; but no being made it, for it is Being itself; it is everything and nothing, and the cause and effect of all. All things originate from *Taou*, conform to *Taou*, and to *Taou* at last they return.

Taou is impalpable. You look at it, and cannot see it. You listen to it, and you cannot hear it. You try to touch it, and you cannot reach it. You use it, and cannot exhaust it. It is not to be expressed in words. It is still and void ; it stands alone and changes not ; it circulates everywhere and is not endangered. It is ever inactive, and yet leaves nothing undone. From it phenomena appear, through it they change, in it they disappear. Formless, it is the cause of form. Nameless, it is the origin of heaven and earth ; with a name, it is the mother of all things. It is the ethical nature of the good man and the principles of his action. If we had then to express the meaning of *Taou*, we should describe it as (1) the Absolute, the totality of Being and Things ; (2) the phenomenal world and its order ; and (3) the ethical nature of the good man and the principle of his action.

The circumlocution with which it is necessary to express the meaning of this one word *Taou* is an illustration of the difficulty of elucidating the obscure and concisely-worded pages of the *Taou-tĭh king.* The subjects of which that work treats, as Mr. Watters very justly remarks, " even when discussed in a clear and plain style and with a rich language, are found to be difficult of elucidation ; and how much more so must they be when discussed in short enigmatical sentences ? Laou-tsze, like all other philosophers who live and write in the infancy of a literary language, had only a very imperfect medium through which to communicate his doctrines. The language of his time was rude and imperfect, utterly unfit to express the deep thoughts of a meditative mind ; and hence it could at best but ' half reveal and half conceal the soul within.' " Its short sentences are doubtless but the texts of the sermons that were preached by the old philosopher to his disciples. To us these *vivâ voce* commentaries and glosses are lost, and only the headings remain.

Like Pythagoras, Laou-tsze was in China the first great awakener and suggester of thought. Unlike Confucius, whose mission it was to revive in a degenerate age the teachings of the ancient Chinese sages, Laou-tsze appears to have drawn his inspirations from abroad. Every part of his system, from its first conception down to its minutest details, is distinctly Brahminical; and the materials for the interpretation of the *Taou-tih king* must therefore be looked for not in the early books of the Chinese, but in the writings of the Indian philosophers, more especially of the Vedanta school.

The obscurity which thus surrounds the writing of Laou-tsze has given rise to many false conceptions of the object which the old philosopher had in view. There is with most people a tendency to seek below the surface for some occult and far-fetched explanation of a difficulty rather than adopt the plain interpretation which lies on the surface before them. To this process Laou-tsze's writings have been very generally subjected. In them, it has been said, are to be traced the outpourings of a misanthrope who advocated an ascetic seclusion from the cares and turmoils of the world as well as from even its sights and sounds. Some have accused him of writing he knew not what, while others, as has been seen, have credited him with having forestalled many of the great truths of Christianity.

An impartial student of his pages, however, will discover that his, like that of Confucius, is a purely politico-ethical system. But unlike Confucius, instead of trying to reform the empire by the imposition of forms and regulations, his object was to lead people back to the state of primitive society before forms were, and before regulations existed. "When the world," said he, "has many prohibitory enactments, the people become more and more poor. When the people have many warlike weapons, the government gets more and more into trouble. The more craft and ingenuity men have, the greater the number of fantastic things that come out. And as works of cunning art are more displayed, thieves multiply." Far from being the misanthrope he is said by some to have been, his writings display a kindly sympathy for his fellow-men, and a yearning desire for their social and political improvement.

Self-abnegation is his cardinal rule for both the sovereign and the people. A running stream is the favourite metaphor he employs to express the ideal course of conduct. While its waters fertilize, cleanse, and refresh, it runs to a place which all disdain. And thus the sage sovereign when he wishes to be above the people, will, by his words, place himself below them. When he wishes to be before the people, he must, in his person, keep behind them. In this way, while he occupies a position above the people, they do not feel his weight, and while he is before the people they suffer no inconvenience. The whole empire, therefore, delights to exalt him, and no one is offended.[1] " Therefore," the Sage says, "he who bears the reproach of his country shall be called the lord of the land, and he who bears the calamities of his country shall be called the king of the world." [2]

It was by such gentle suasion as this that he would govern the empire and recall men from the sway of the fierce passions which had been aroused by princely jealousies, base tyrannies, and unruly violence, to a state of primitive simplicity, when the " Great Taou " was the rule of life, and before philanthropy and justice had acquired names ; when perfect concord reigned in families, and before filial piety and fatherly compassion began ; when the State was perfectly ordered, and before patriots were known.[3] Continuing the same train of thought, Laou-tsze directs an attack against the Confucianists, the Pharisees of the age. " Abandon your wisdom," said he, " and cast away your prudence, and the people will be a hundred-fold more happy. Renounce your philanthropy, and throw aside your justice, and the people will return to filial piety and fatherly compassion. Renounce your cleverness, and forego your gains, and thieves will disappear. . . . And appear in your own unadorned simplicity, preserve your purity, curb your selfishness, and curtail your ambitious desires."[4]

But though Laou-tsze thus condemned some of the teachings of Confucius, he endorsed others. It is repeatedly laid down in the *Shoo King* that a truly virtuous sovereign who is served by upright minis-

[1] Chap. lxvi.
[2] Chap. lxxviii.
[3] Chap. xviii.
[4] Chap. xix.

ters will by the force of his example produce an effect upon his people, which neither the enactment of laws nor the infliction of punishment will be able to accomplish. And to this condition he desired to see his distracted country return. On the loud-mouthed politicians who raised their voices at every street-corner to proclaim their own wisdom and the wickedness of their adversaries, he sought to impress the lesson that in much speaking there was much folly, and that it was better to keep the lips closed than to talk with a glib tongue; that many meddlers only further add to the entanglements of the State, which it should be the duty of every true citizen to help to unravel; and that the glare of factious politics could be tempered only by the exercise of modesty and self-emptiness.[1]

Thus it was in the days of old, to which he is as fond of referring as was Confucius. Then those who practised *Taou* sought not to make the people clever, but to make them simple, not to encourage them in hyprocrisy and fraud, but to teach them the true virtues of honesty and unselfishness. Such men were blessings to their countries and honours to the world.[2] But in his day, he complains that men gave up the substance and followed after the shadow. They claimed the possession of virtues of which they had but the outside veneer. "As for me," said Laou-tsze, "I have three precious things which I hold fast and prize; namely, compassion, economy, and humility. Being compassionate I can be brave, being economical I can be liberal, and being humble I can

[1] Chap. lvi. [2] Chap. lxv.

become the chief of men. But in the present day men give up compassion, and cultivate only courage; they give up economy, and aim only at liberality; they give up the last place, and seek only the first: it is their death. Compassion is that which is victorious in the attack and secure in the defence. When Heaven would save a man, it encircles him with compassion."

In such utterances as these Laou-tsze showed himself to be as superior to Confucius as the Christian dispensation is to the Mosaic law. Confucius would have the outside of the platter cleansed: he would have every rite and ceremony, whether at court, in official life, or within the family circle, scrupulously observed, down to the number of meals to be eaten, and the posture to be assumed in bed. But Laou-tsze went deeper, and drawing an analogy from the unalterable law of nature, under which in all created things there take place constantly-recurring alternations from strength to weakness, and from weakness to strength, he taught the lesson which has been consecrated by Christ, that "he who exalteth himself shall be abased, and he who humbleth himself shall be exalted." "He who knows the light, and at the same time keeps the shade, will be the whole world's model. Being the whole world's model, eternal virtue will not miss him, and he will return home to the Absolute. He who knows the glory, and at the same time keeps to shame, will be the whole world's valley. Being the whole world's valley, eternal virtue will fill him, and he will return home to *Taou*."[1]

· Chap. xxviii.

Laou-tsze held with Confucius that man's nature was good, and that he who avoided the snare of the world, and acted in all things in conformity with the uncontaminated instincts of that nature, would possess *Taou*, and would eventually return home to *Taou*. It is the wisdom of this world, it is the knowledge of good and evil, which is the ruin of man. Let him but return to an age of primitive simplicity, when he finds the highest pleasure and contentment in the comforts of his home, when he eats the fruit of the labour of his hands, when he knows no wants, and is disturbed by no cares, and he will then fulfil the duties of a man and of a citizen in their highest sense. Better that he should be ignorant than that he should possess this world's wisdom; better that he should use knotted cords to express his thoughts than that he should have the pen of a Confucius;[1] better that he should be still and retiring than that he should be restless and striving. The philosophers of old were timid, like one crossing a stream; they were cautious, like one who dreads his neighbour; they were circumspect, like a man from home; they effaced themselves, like ice that is about to melt; they were simple, like unwrought wood; they were vacant, like a valley; they were dim, like muddy water.[2] Therefore their reward was long life, and their virtue was complete.

But the days of a man who strives must necessarily be short. A violent wind will not outlast the morning, neither will a pouring rain outlast the day.[3]

---

[1] Chap. lxxx.   [2] Chap. xv.   [3] Chap. xxiii.

And so with all human effort, the greater it is the
less enduring it will be. Heaven and earth do not
aim after life; therefore heaven is long, and earth is
lasting. The sage puts himself last, and is therefore
first; he abandons himself, and is therefore preserved.[1] It is better, therefore, to rest contented
than to strive after fulness. As when gold and gems
fill a hall none can protect them, so wealth and
honour with pride bring their own punishment.[2] For
there is no solidity about these things; they are but
an outward show, and possess none of the reality
which belongs to *Taou*. Thus it is that when *Taou*
is lost, then comes virtue; when virtue is lost, then
comes benevolence; when benevolence is lost, then
comes justice; and when justice is lost, then comes
propriety. For propriety is the mere skeleton of
fidelity and faith, and the precursor of confusion.[3]

To bring the people back to this state of Arcadian
simplicity should be the main object of the sovereign.
Their good must be his chief and only care, and as
it rests within his power to confer every blessing
upon them, so the responsibility belongs to him of
every evil which overtakes them. Everything for the
people, and everything by the people, is the maxim
of his very undespotic government. The ruler
receives the appointment of Heaven, and the people
endorse the election. As long as he remains faithful
to his trust, and obedient to the dictates of his ideal
nature, his throne is secure to him; but the same
powers that make can unmake; and if he fall away

[1] Chap. vii.   [2] Chap. ix.   [3] Chap. xxviii.

from *Taou*, the countenance of Heaven will be withdrawn, and the people will throw off their allegiance to him. Thus it is that "nobles regard the commonalty as their origin, and men of high estate look upon what is ignoble as their foundation and support. This is the reason why kings and princes style themselves 'orphans,' 'lonely men,' and 'men devoid of virtue.' Is not this an acknowledgment that they are rooted in their inferiors? Deny it! Why, a cart taken to pieces is no cart. A sage does not wish to be esteemed as jade, nor to be treated with contempt as a stone."

A wise ruler will remember that "a nation is a growth, not a manufacture," and that the spiritual weapons of this world cannot be formed by laws and regulations. He will strive, therefore, to empty the hearts of his subjects, and to fill their stomachs; to weaken their wills, and to strengthen their bones; to keep the people from the desire and the knowledge of evil, and to keep in subjection those who have tasted of the tree of the knowledge of good and evil. He will act inaction, and so nothing will be ungoverned.[1] This is all that is required to secure the greatest amount of happiness to a people. Prohibitory enactments and constant intermeddling in political and social matters merely tend to produce the evils they are intended to avert. If the ruler do but love quietness, avoid law-making, and be free from lusts, everything will spontaneously submit to him; heaven and earth will combine to send down

---

[1] Chap. iii.

upon him refreshing dew, and the people will of themselves harmonize together.[1] To interfere with the freedom of the people is to deny the existence of *Taou* in their midst, and to make them the slaves of rules rather than the freemen of principles. It was thus that the rulers of antiquity governed their kingdoms, and in those "brave days of old" so light were the hands that held the reins that the people only knew of the existence of their superiors. But in the next age, when sovereigns began to pass as sages, they became attached to them and flattered them. In the next, when they began to boast of wisdom, the people dreaded them; and, last of all, when they talked of benevolence and justice; the people despised them. Thus the people lost all the naturally controlling influences which had been inherent in them, and became dependent on laws and regulations for the maintenance of their virtue. But as these, when *Taou* is lost, are as phantoms, leading men farther and farther from the right way, the people gradually fell lower and lower in the social scale, until the country reached the state of disorganization and ruin which existed in his day.

The violence of unruly men was the main feature of that period. The wildest passions, instigated by ambition and fostered by greed, were let loose upon society. No rights were recognised and no institutions were held sacred by men who sought only their own selfish ends at the expense of others. War and strife, rapine and plunder, were rife throughout the land.

[1] Chap. xxxii.

Princes, disregarding the true welfare and the necessary protection of their subjects, enforced levies, re-
quisitioned supplies, and marched their armies
through the standing crops to meet their enemies
beyond their frontiers, leaving behind them a remnant
of the people ruined by their exactions and rendered
desperate by want. No wonder, then, that the man
who had resigned his office as Keeper of the Archives
at the court of Chow, rather than sanction by his
presence the iniquities perpetrated by the sovereign
of that State, raised his voice with vehemence against
the wild violence of the time, against the sin of
giving rein to desire, against the misery of discon-
tent, and against the dire calamities entailed by the
desire of possessing.[1]

Looking around on the untilled lands and deserted
homesteads of his native State, he points out that
where legions are quartered, briers and thorns grow,
and that in the track of large armies follow want and
famine.[2] Instead of the grain-bearing fields ploughed
by farm-horses, are waste commons used for breeding
and rearing war-horses.[3] Ploughshares are converted
into those " instruments of ill-omen," the weapons of
war. The left hand, the weak side, which in times
of peace is considered the place of honour, is deserted
for the side of the strong right hand, with which warriors deal death and destruction around them. To
be on the side of peace is but to earn contempt from
men whose greatest boast is that they have trodden
underfoot their enemies and robbed them of their
lands and treasures.

[1] Chap. xlvi. [2] Chap. xxx. [3] Chap. xlvi.

How different to this is the conduct of a superior man. Peace is his highest aim, and the life of his fellow-creatures is his highest care. He takes up his weapon as a last resource only, when every other expedient has failed, and fights bravely, but only when it is to effect some good purpose. " He ventures nothing for the sake of power. He strikes a decisive blow at the right time, but does not boast of his success. He strikes a decisive blow and does not pride himself on it : He strikes a decisive blow and is not puffed up." On the contrary, he mourns over the destruction of human life with bitter tears, and lays down his arms as soon as the necessity of using them is past. After the campaign is over, he takes his place on the right, as though he were at a funeral, for he feels that he has been instrumental in destroying the lives of his fellow-men, and he desires to mourn over their deaths.[1] A truly great general is no lover of war, nor is he revengeful and passionate. He orders the battle, but prefers not to lead the van ; he would rather await the attack than lead the assault. If all men were thus minded, there would be no rushing into the ranks ; there would be no baring the arm, as those eager for the fight ; there would be no charging the enemy in reckless haste, and there would be no grasping of weapons until the enemy were upon them. A good general never lightly engages in a war, for he knows well that there is no surer way of losing one's treasure than this. And therefore it is that when opposing warriors join in battle, the compassionate is always the conqueror.[2]

[1] Chap. xxxi.   [2] Chap. lxix.

In the same spirit, when he returns after the con-clusion of a victorious peace, he knows full well that there must remain some ill-feeling against him, and he therefore lets matters rest. He fulfils his part of the treaty and exacts nothing from the other side. He attends only to his own promises and his own claims.[1] If after this sort the people of a country were governed and led, though they might have armour they would have no occasion to put it on, and the deadly peril which follows the display of warlike weapons as surely as death overtakes the fish which is taken out of the water, would be avoided.

Laou-tsze's utterances on these points contain words of wisdom for all time, and apply with equal force to the kingdoms of the Western world at the present day as to the States of China two thousand years ago. Within the last few years we have seen wars "lightly" undertaken, which have ended in the "cost of treasure" to the aggressor. We have seen oppressive terms of peace made, which have left behind a bitter sense of wrong; and we have seen advantage taken of a fallen foe which has ended in disaster to the conqueror. It may possibly be thought that in many ways Laou-tsze's ideals are impracticable and unsuited for the very material world about us. But the times in which he lived were exceptionally disordered, the evils of which we have only but a faint idea from the records handed down to us, were flourishing around him on every

Chap. lxxix.

side. With his own eyes he saw the misery created
by the restless ambition of the princes and the un-
restrained licentiousness of the people. "Alas!" said
he, "the people will never cease from their madness,
but are full of ambitious desires." For such a state
of things an heroic remedy was, in his opinion, necessary. Confucius had thought to embody the teachings of the ancient sages in a minute ritual, and had
failed. Laou-tsze strove to set aside all forms and
ceremonies and to get behind them to the principles
on which they rested, and he also failed. In troublous
times, when men's passions have broken loose, and
the law of "every man for himself" is supreme, a
teacher who desires to check the pursuit of selfish
aims and of personal aggrandisement must have
some compensating benefit to offer in exchange for
the self-sacrifice entailed in foregoing schemes which
present a prospect of immediate and substantial advantage. But neither of them had any more tempt-
ing promise to hold out than that virtue is its own
reward. It is true that Laou-tsze promises to the
man who follows *Taou* that he shall gain such an
insight into the workings of *Taou* as is withheld
from him who has not conquered his passions; that
he shall see the small beginnings of things, and
shall possess a light which shall bring him home to
its own brightness; that he shall be "like an infant
whom poisonous reptiles will not sting, wild beasts
will not seize, and birds of prey will not strike";
that his days shall be prolonged in the land, not by
watching carefully over his own welfare, but by disregarding every selfish interest; and when, in the

fulness of years, death at last comes, he need fear
no evil, for he is in no danger of perishing. As he
comes forth from *Taou* so he will return to *Taou,*
and will endure as long as *Taou* endures or as
heaven lasts : with delight the eternal mother of all
things will receive him into herself, and he will return
home to a still eternity.

The same reasons which made Laou-tsze an enemy
to war and all violence, rendered him opposed to
capital punishment. But in addition to this he held
that if a State were well governed the necessity for
capital, or indeed, any other punishment, could not
arise. If the people could be taught to love simplicity and purity, crime would cease to exist. But it is
the striving after wealth, learning, and position which
disorders men's minds, rouses their passions, and
causes them to think lightly of death. By a people
who are addicted to pleasure and to the gratification
of their passions, life is never highly esteemed. It is
only by those who recognise in life a serious purpose,
and have a firm faith in a future existence, that it is
invested with a real value. Men who live only for
amusement, or for the indulgence of their selfish
caprices, are willing enough to resign their being when
their appetites fail them, from whatever cause, and
when their ambitious schemes fall to the ground. And
when once a people has reached this stage of recklessness, no punishment will be effectual to prevent their
rushing into sin. " When the people do not fear
death, to what purpose is death still used to overcome them ? " But if there be a man worthy of death,
there is always the " Great Executioner " in whose

hands are the issues of life and death. Whom he will he slays, and whom he will he keepeth alive; and who is man that he should interfere between the evil-doer and his judge? "Now for any man to act the executioner's part is to hew out the Great Architect's work for him. And he who undertakes to hew for the Great Architect rarely fails to cut his hands."

But Laou-tsze goes beyond this and says, "Judge not your fellow-men. Be content to know yourself. Be chaste, but do not chasten others. Be strictly correct yourself, and do not cut and carve other people. And learn not to impute wickedness to the unfortunate. If one man dies and another is preserved alive, why point at either of them as the object of Heaven's hatred? A truly good man loves all men and rejects none, he respects all things and rejects nothing; he associates with good men and interchanges instruction with them, but bad men are the materials on which he works, and to bring such back to *Taou* is the great object of his life. But he "who honours not his instructor, and he who loves not his material, though accounted wise, are greatly deluded."

CHAPTER III.

THE TAOU TIH KING (*continued*).

ON the subject of ethics Laou-tsze speaks out plainly;
but in forming an estimate of the moral worth of his
maxims it is again necessary to remember that he
was less a general teacher, though much that he
taught applies to the world at large, than a protestant
against the particular vices of his time. He saw men
ambitious and violent, and to such he preached
modesty and self-restraint; he saw men greedy in the
pursuit of gain, and licentious, and for the benefit of
such he advocated the virtues of self-abnegation and
continence. But here he stopped. Of courage, truth,
and honesty he says little, and in this respect appears
to fall short of Confucius, who laid great stress on
these virtues. Possibly Laou-tsze was content to
know that the greater included the less, and that if
he could persuade men to be modest, self-denying,
and virtuous, there would be no need to preach to
them of either truth, honesty, or courage. But if he
fell behind Confucius in this, he far surpassed him
when he proclaimed the golden rule of Christianity,
" Recompense evil with good."[1]   To this level

Chap. lxiii.

Confucius deliberately refused to rise, and when asked his opinion on the sentiment expressed by his contemporary, his matter-of-fact mind failed, as we have seen, to comprehend that great maxim.

Like Confucius, Laou-tsze speaks of his ideal man as the Sage. In him resides every virtue. He is magnanimous, he is catholic, he is the equal of heaven, he is the embodiment of *Taou*, and eternity is his.[1] To reach this lofty state should be the desire and object of all men, and to this end they should be modest and retiring, not making themselves great, and thus they will be able to achieve greatness. To know others is to be wise, but he who knows himself is enlightened. He who overcomes others is strong, but he who conquers himself is mighty. He who has a contented mind is rich. He who acts with energy has a purpose. He who does not act contrary to his nature continues long, and he who dies and perishes not enjoys eternity.[2]

Among men it is common to respect the strong and to despise the weak. But they forget that out of weakness comes forth strength, and that the tender things of this world overcome the hard. Of all the weak things in the world nothing exceeds water, and yet beyond all those who attack hard and strong things it is superior. Does not the soft and flexible creeper tyrannize over and sometimes destroy the strong tree round which it twines? And what rock is

Chap. xvi.   [2] Ibid. xxxiii.

there which is able to withstand the constant dripping
of water?   All the difficult things in this world must
originate in what is easy, and the great things must all
spring from what is small.   " The sage therefore never
attempts what is great, and hence is able to accomplish
great things.   He who lightly assents will rarely keep
his word, and he who has many easy things will have
many difficulties.   Therefore the sage views things as
difficult, and never has any difficulty."   In other words,
he foresees the evil day coming, and by careful watch-
fulness provides against it.   He recollects that the
tree which fills the arms grew from a slender twig, and
that the castle of nine stories was raised from a mound
of earth ; and he therefore grapples with his business
before it has taken form, and regulates affairs before
disorder comes.   That which is brittle is easy broken,
and that which is minute is easily dispersed.   He is
as careful in finishing a matter as he is in beginning
it, and therefore always brings it to a successful
issue.[1]

A man who is wise, therefore, will guard against the
small beginnings of evil, whether in his own heart or
in the world around him, and will thus achieve great
things.   He will destroy the seed, and thus demolish
the huge forest tree which would otherwise grow from
it.   He will abase himself, and thus avoid the crush-
ing defeats to which overweening pride is subjected.
He will humble himself, and so shall be preserved
entire ; he will bend himself, and so shall be
straightened ; he will abase himself, and so shall be

[1] Chap. lxiv.

filled ; he will diminish himself, and so shall succeed.[1]
He will empty himself of passions, and will then
behold the spiritual essence of *Taou.*   He will carefully keep "the inner man," and shall thus return
home entire to his origin.   He will attach himself to
what is real, and throw on one side what is merely
showy and superficial.   He will cherish compassion,
economy, and humility.[2]

In the eyes of Laou-tsze, as well as of Confucius, a
glib talker was a suspected person.   A man on tiptoe
cannot stand still, and so a man who is always seeking prominence in talking, as in other things, cannot
remain quiet and self-contained.   Shut your lips, is
his advice, and close the portals of your eyes and
ears, and as long as you live you will have no trouble ;
but open your lips and meddle with things, and as
long as you live you will multiply difficulties.[3]   The
great object of every man should be to possess himself, and this can only be done by avoiding all excesses,
and gaiety, and splendour.   A man who is self-dis-
playing does not really shine; he who is self-approving
is not held in esteem ; he who is self-praising has no
merit ; and he who is self-exalting does not stand
high.

Learning finds no more favour at the hands of Laou-
tsze than with the Quietists.   By both alike it is condemned and contemned.   It is the enemy of that
simplicity and innocence which are the truest
ornaments of a nation.   In the days of old when
sovereigns possessed *Taou,* and when they ruled over

Chap. xxii.   [2] Ibid. lxvii.   [3] Ibid.

P

a peaceful and contented empire, they strove not to make people bright, but to make them simple,—not to encourage wisdom, but to make them content.[1] They recognised that in much learning there was much vexation, that education gave rise to an unhealthy and injurious activity, and that while men disputed about the use of words they forgot the difference between good and evil.[2]   The highest kind of knowledge is to be gained without going beyond one's own door; indeed, the farther a man goes away the less he has of that supreme knowledge, the knowledge of himself. "There is no occasion even as much as to peep through the window to see celestial *Taou*,"[3] and the more men seek after knowledge the further they wander from that state of primitive simplicity which existed in the golden age of the world, when men followed without effort the instincts of their pure and holy nature.   If knowledge of any kind were needed it would be to govern a kingdom, but a kingdom is best governed when left alone.   If the ruler but love quietness, and be free from lusts, the people will walk in the path of righteousness, and will of themselves become simple-minded.[4]   But happiness is ever built up on the back of misery, and misery is ever lurking under happiness.   It is easy, therefore, for a ruler, by want of discretion, by ruthlessly interfering with the freedom of the people, or by educational activity, to bring disaster upon them.   A sage might govern the world without trouble, for he knows how to be mode-

---

[1] Chap. lxv.   [2] Ibid. xx.
[3] Ibid. xlvii.   [4] Ibid. lvii.

rate; not clever, humble; not learned, and still, not active.

"He who regards his greatest fulness as emptiness may employ himself without exhaustion. His greatest uprightness.is as want of rectitude. His greatest skill is as stupidity. His greatest eloquence is as stammering. Activity conquers cold, and quietness conquers heat; but there is a purity and quietude by which one may rule the whole world."[1]

Of a personal God Laou-tsze knew nothing, as far as we may judge from the *Taou-tih king;* and indeed a belief in such a being would be in opposition to the whole tenour of his philosophy. There is no room for a supreme God in his system, as is shown by the only mention he makes of a heavenly ruler. "*Taou,*" he says, "is empty; in operation, exhaustless. In its depth it scans the future of all things. It blunts sharp angles. It unravels disorders. It softens the glare. It shares the dust. In tranquillity it seems ever to remain. I know not whose son it is. It appears to have been before God."[2] *Taou* is Unconditioned Being, which, as an abstraction too subtle for words, is the origin of heaven and earth, including God himself, and when capable of being expressed by name, is the mother of all things.[3]

Like a loving parent, it watches with a providential care over all created beings. From its portals they issued forth into life, and through all the changes and chances of existence it continues on their right hand and on their left, nourishing in love, imparting life to

[1] Chap. xlv. [2] Ibid. iv. [3] Ibid. i.

all, and refusing none. Though before all, above all, and in all, it yet assumes no authority, and though all things submit to it, it does not regard itself as their master.[1] Though it completes, cherishes, and covers all things, it makes no display of strength, but accepts weakness as its characteristic. It does not strive with man. Those who possess it find in it a beneficent and almighty protector, but those who spurn it are left to find out for themselves the folly of their way. " Lay hold of the great form of *Taou*, and the whole world will go to you. It will go to you, and will suffer no injury ; and its rest and peace will be glorious."[2] Even during lifetime it is possible to possess oneself of *Taou*, and the creature may thus become identified with the creator through the annihilation of self.

It is impossible not to recognise the resemblance between the return to *Taou* and the entrance of the Buddhists into Nirvana. But there is this important difference between the two, that whereas the entrance into Nirvana is the extinction of existence, the return to *Taou* is but the recall of the finite to the infinite the creature to the creator.

As far as the *Taou-tih king* furnishes evidence, Laou-tsze had only a shadowy faith in spirits, and those he recognised were of an inferior kind, such as bow before the presence of one who follows *Taou*. Like Confucius, he held that the Sage had rule over the spirits of the world. Let but a Sage, therefore, sit upon the throne, and the reflection of his

[1] Chap. xxxiv.   Ibid. xxxv.

virtue will cause the demons to hide their diminished heads, and this, not because they lack the power for mischief, but because evil can never conquer right.[1]

His was not a spiritual religion, but was a species of Mysticism, begotten of heart-weariness at the hopeless prospect he saw before him in his country, and of an ardent longing for that repose which he found it impossible to secure among men whose one object in life was to secure their own advantage at all hazards and in defiance of all right. For years he communed with his own heart, and was still; but at last the spirit burned within him, and he gave vent to his heart-searching protest against the literalism, hypocrisy, formality, and scholasticism of his time. He had no compliments to exchange with men like Confucius, who paraded their virtue before the world, and boasted of the excellence of their words and deeds. In his eyes, " one pure act of internal resignation was more worth than a hundred thousand exercises of one's own will." And who will not say that he was right?

As has already been stated, Laou-tsze's was primarily a politico-ethical system. So he himself regarded it, and so it was treated by his immediate followers. But whether it was the outcome of a deeper speculative belief on the origin and nature of the universe, or whether it led up to it, we have scattered throughout the *Taou-tih-king* evidence that Laou-tsze had established in his own mind a complete theory on the existence of the material world and the constitution of man.

---

[1] Chap. lx.

According to him, all existing beings came forth from *Taou*, the " abyss mother," the " mother of all things." In the beginning was *Taou*, and when as yet it was an abstraction, inexpressible in words, he regarded it as potential existence, or, as he expresses it elsewhere, as non-existence. " From this point of view it is imperceptible to man, and can be spoken of only negatively ; and so such terms as non-existence, the unlimited or infinite, the non-exerting, the matterless, are the expressions used with reference to *Taou* so considered." [1] It is thus the equivalent of chaos, and is the beginning of heaven and earth. With this creation it passes from potential to actual existence, and out of non-existence comes existence. But whether as potential or actual existence, it is yet *Taou*, and existence and non-existence are regarded as one, for though *two* phenominally, they are *one* nominally. Considered as potential existence, *Taou* is " empty," " calm," " void," " shapeless," and " immaterial." " Above it is not bright, below it is not obscure. Boundless in its operation, it cannot be named. Returning it goes home into nothing. This I call the appearance of non-appearance, the form of nothingness. This is what baffles investigation." [2] It is invisible, inaudible, and unreachable. At the same time, it contains potentially all life, form, and substance, and from it proceed all created things, the heaven above, the earth beneath, and all the inhabitants of the earth.

But it does more than create. It watches over its

Watter's " Lao-tzŭ," p. 46.   [2] Chap. xiv.

offspring with the fondness of a parent. It enters into the life of each individual thing; it penetrates the impenetrable; it produces, nourishes, enlarges, feeds, completes, ripens, cherishes, and covers all things. It is the good man's glory and the bad man's hope.[1] It exalts the humble and abases the pride of the lofty. It equalises the careers of men, taking from him who has a superabundance and giving to him who wants.[2] It blesses those who help others in adversity, and gives a double portion to those who supply the wants of the needy.[3] But though all-pervading, it works unseen; though ever inactive, it leaves nothing undone. It is everything and nothing; it is the smallest possible quantity and yet the whole. It is the unity of the universe, and as such supports, strengthens, and nourishes all created things.

The first chapter of the *Taou-tih-king* tells us that "that which is nameless is the beginning of heaven and earth," and elsewhere we are let into the secret of the processes which led up to this creation. Taou produced one, the first great cause; one produced two, the male and female principles of nature; two produced three; and three produced all things beginning with heaven and earth. Heaven is treated by Laou-tsze much in the same way as by Confucius, but with far more reserve. In the utterances of both teachers we find the word used to designate the material heaven as well as a personified heaven. Just as Confucius speaks of the Sage as being the

---

[1] Chap. lxii.　　　[2] Ibid. lxxvii.　　　[3] Ibid. lxxxi.

equal of heaven, Laou-tsze says that he is the associate of heaven, and that he is heaven itself.[1] Heaven, also according to him, gives laws to the earth just as it takes its law from *Taou*.[2] It has no special love, but regards all existing beings as grass-dogs made for sacrificial rites, *i.e.*, for temporary purposes. It is as unselfish as it is impartial, and because it does not aim at life it lasts long. It is great and compassionate, and is ever ready to become the saviour of men. But it is also the material heaven, and maintains its existence by the " clearness " which is imparted to it by its unity with *Taou*.

Earth is treated much in the same way. It is inferior to heaven both as a personality and as part of the material universe, but it is associated with heaven in its existence and in its relation to man. As the material earth it is preserved from the danger of falling to pieces by its unity with *Taou*.

Next to issue fresh from the teaming womb of *Taou* were all created things, thus illustrating the eternal law of constant alternation from strength to weakness and back again to strength, which is common to all nature. Existence and non-existence mutually originate each other; so also difficulty and ease, long and short, high and low, treble and bass, before and after.[3] Man also, who in his life is supple and tender, in his death is rigid and strong. And so with all things. When shrubs and trees which in their life are weak and tender become withered and tough it is a sign of their decay. When the tree has become

---

[1] Chap. xvi.   [2] Ibid. xxv.   [3] Ibid. ii.

strong it is cut down. Thus that which is strong is laid low, and that which is weak and tender is lifted up.[1] The heavy is the root of the light. The still is the ruler of the moving.[2]

All things endure for a set time and then perish. Together they came into being, and to each is allotted a certain period of growth and maturity, but when the highest point of vigour has been reached it straightway becomes old and returns home to its root. " This is said to be a reversion to destiny." Emptiness is the only thing which endures, and this is at the same time of the highest use. The space between heaven and earth, for example, may be likened to a pair of bellows, which though it is empty never collapses, and which the more it is exercised the more it brings forth. So also with the wheel of a carriage, or an earthen vessel, or the windows and doors of a house. In each case it is the non-existing or empty part which is useful. The spokes and nave of the wheel, the walls of the earthen vessel, and the frames of the doors and windows are advantageous, but the use of each depends on the part which is empty. " So then existence may be said to correspond to gain, but non-existence to use."[3] When a thing is to be weakened it must first be strengthened ; when it is about to be brought low, it must first be raised up ; and that which is to be taken away from it must first be given to it.[4]

In the superiority of non-existence over existence

---

[1] Chap. lxxvi.

[2] Ibid. xxvi.

[3] Ibid. xi.

[4] Ibid. xxxvi.

lies the lesson which above all others Laou-tsze desired to impress on man. The great concern of all men in all ages has been to take care of the things of the body and to neglect the cultivation of the inner man ; to seek after the gratification of sense, and to forget the importance of the soul. And what is the result ? The five colours which so delight the eyes not unfrequently produce blindness. The five sounds which so enchant the ear are often the cause of deafness. A man's palate which at first revels in the five tastes soon loses all sense of flavour. The pursuit of pleasure or of ambition is equally deceptive. Riding and hunting will drive a man mad, and things hard to procure bring evil upon their possessors. "Therefore the sage makes provision for the inner man and not for his eyes. He puts aside the one that he may take the other in hand."[1] He remembers that rest is the lord of motion, and never allows himself to depart from a state of quietude and gravity.[2]

Such is a sketch of the doctrine set forth by Laou-tsze in the *Taou-tih-king*. It is an old-world belief and finds many parallels in the eastern and western worlds. Thus it is interesting as showing that the contemplation of the same objects of supreme importance to man has been attended by the same results among the quick-witted Greeks, the subtle-minded Hindoos, and the prosaic Chinamen. We know so little of Laou-tsze's history that it is impossible to say whether or no he drew his inspiration directly from India. It is possible that he did, but whether this be

---

[1] Chap. xii.   [2] Ibid. xxvi.

so or not, the resemblance between the leading characteristics of Hindoo mysticism and those of Taouism
are sufficiently striking. When we are told that Hindoo mysticism "lays claim to disinterested love, as
opposed to a mercenary religion; that it reacts
against the ceremonial prescriptions and pedantic
literature of the Vedas; that it identifies, in its
Pantheism, subject and object, worshipper and worshipped; that it aims at ultimate absorption into the
infinite; that it inculcates as the way to this dissolu-
tion absolute passivity, withdrawal into the inmost
self, and cessation of all the powers; that it believes
that eternity may thus be realized in time; that it
has its mythical miraculous pretensions, i.e., its the-
urgic department";[1] we see reflected as in a glass
the various stages through which Taouism has passed
from the time it was first conceived in the mind of
Laou-tsze down to its latest superstitious developments.

To the many and gross evils which have grown out
of his system, Laou-tsze gave no countenance whatever.
His was no superstitious faith, but was an abstract
belief in an infinite essence, and though it is true that
his teachings have led to the pantheistic identification
of the creature with the creator, and that some of his
utterances have been held to countenance the systems
of charms and elixirs which have disgraced the religion
in later times, yet the *Taou-tih-king* stands forth as
an undeniable witness to prove that its author was
singularly free from all taint of such superstitions,

[1] Vaughan's " Hours with the Mystics."

and that nothing could be more opposed to the humility and self-emptiness which he preached with all sincerity than his own apotheosis, nor to his hatred of deception than the magical arts of his degenerate followers. His system was transcendental, but it was pure, and in rules of general morality he fell behind no heathen philosopher which the world has seen, and he far surpassed them all when he communicated that maxim which has been one of the great glories of Christianity: "Recompense evil with good."

CHAPTER IV.

LEIH-TSZE AND CHWANG-TSZE.

BUT the same fate which has overtaken the systems of the founders of all religions was speedily to befall the doctrines of Laou-tsze. No doctrine however pure, not even Christianity itself, has been able everywhere to maintain its purity. After the disappearance of the founder whose personal influence serves to maintain the religious standard he has established, and to whom all questions arising on disputed points may be referred, there remain but the records of his deeds and words. How soon the study of these may give rise to disputations and heresies, let the history of Christianity bear testimony. But among the Taouists these never obtained any firm hold among the followers of Laou-tsze. He had shown forth no mighty deeds, he had shunned the centres of concourse, his life had not been marked by any supernatural manifestations, nor by any notable acts of either power or self-devotion, and of the manner of his death nothing is known. His was a life of retired meditation, and the direction which in his many years of seclusion his thoughts took was foreign to the preconceived ideas and tone of the national mind. His ideas also had to compete with those of a formidable rival in the person of Confucius, who paraded the country followed by a crowd of disciples, associating with kings and princes, and preaching the glories of his native land and the incomparable excellence of the ancient rulers of China.

Far more likely to attract were the sayings and doings of Confucius, which sounded pleasantly in the ears of a people already proud of the history of their country, and which attracted the attention of all men. Already the ground was prepared for the reception of the seed he was to cast upon it, and when in due time the harvest began to appear there was shown forth a goodly crop of the rich and great, the powerful and the wise.   But on the other hand Taouism was as the cave of Adullam, a retreat to which all those who were discontented with their lots, and who despaired of the future of their country, took refuge.   Such men were by no means the best depositories of the teachings of Laou-tsze.   The genial tone and kindly thoughts of the " old philosopher " became transformed under their hands into sneers and complaints, and his philosophy of existence was converted into arguments in support of a careless indifference of life and of death.

Conspicuous among the early writers on Taouism are Lieh Yü-kow, commonly known as Lieh-tsze, and Chwang Chow, who is usually spoken of as Chwang-tsze.   The first of these was born in the 5th century B.C., in the generation immediately succeeding that of Confucius and of Laou-tsze, and his writings fairly represent the tone which had already begun to be

taken up concerning the doctrines of his master.
The belief in the identity of existence and non-existence, and the constant alternations from one to
the other observable in all nature, assumed in the eyes
of Lieh-tsze a warrant for the old doctrine, " Let us
eat and drink, for to-morrow we die." " Why trouble
oneself," he asks, "about anything in life? Is not death,
which is but a return from existence to non-existence,
ever close at hand ? My body is not my own ; I am
merely an inhabitant of it for the time being, and shall
resign it when I return to the ' Abyss Mother.' Why,
then, should I weary myself in the pursuit of politics
or of the many anxieties with which some men delight
to perplex themselves? Rather let me ' take the
goods the gods provide' and enjoy to-day, leaving the
morrow to take care of itself."

In this spirit he quotes with approval the account of
an interview between Confucius and a follower of Laou-
tsze named Ying, whom Confucius met wearing a leather
girdle about his loins in the fields near the city of Ching,
and who was solacing his loneliness by singing to his
guitar. " Sir, what makes you so cheerful ? " asked
Confucius. "I have indeed many causes for rejoicing," answered Ying. " Of all the things created
by Heaven, are not human beings the most honourable?
And I am a human being. That is one cause for
rejoicing. Are not men noble and women contempti-
ble ? And I am a man. That is a second cause for
rejoicing. Again, are not some men born who never
see the light of the sun or moon, and who never live
to get out of swaddling-clothes? I have walked the
earth for ninety years. That is a third cause for

rejoicing. Poverty is the normal condition of scholars and death comes to all, why should I mourn because I live as others, and because I shall die like them?" "Good," said Confucius; "you are indeed wise."[1]

A dream is the common medium adopted by Lieh-tsze for picturing ideal states of society, and thus he relates that the Emperor Hwang-te, after a long fast undertaken to subdue his lascivious propensities, fell asleep and dreamt that he was transported without effort into a far country, where the people were without rulers, for they were masters of themselves,—were without passion, for they controlled their desires. They regarded life without pleasure and death without dread, and therefore were overtaken by no untimely fates. They knew neither relations nor connections, and so were free from love and hate. Rebellion and sycophancy were unknown among them, and therefore they suffered no injury. There was nothing they either loved or cared for, and there was nothing they either reverenced or feared. They walked in water without being drowned, they threw themselves into the fire without being burnt, and they might be cut and struck without receiving hurt. They mounted into the air and walked as on the ground. They slept in space as though they were on their beds, and the clouds and the mists interfered with them not. They listened to the thunder and were not deafened. They saw beauty and ugliness, and their hearts remained firm. Mountains and valleys presented no

[1] Chun heu chin king. Keuen I.

obstacles to them, for they walked on the paths of the gods. And so he awoke.[1]

In this allegory we have foreshadowed the gross superstitions which were soon to reduce the pure imaginings of Laou-tsze to the level of Shamanism. The doctrines taught by Laou-tsze, of the possible absorption of the creature into the Creator had already given rise to the pantheistic belief that even in this present life it was possible for men to become gods, and if gods, that then they were superior to the laws of nature. On this subject Leih-tsze questioned the keeper of the pass to whom Laou-tsze had given his Taou-tih king. At first Yin He was disinclined to answer, but at last admitted that men might walk in the air, and venture into fire without being burnt; but he added, "This sort comes only with the possession of a perfectly pure spirit, and is not to be acquired by art."

Leih-tsze, however, thought otherwise, and relates as facts wondrous tales of the adventures of Muh Wang, who by the aid of a magician from the West visited fairy-land, and made the acquaintance of the deity known as the Se wang moo, or Western Royal Mother. But he goes further, and states that a certain Laou Ching-tsze learnt from Yin He himself the arts of creating and of conjuring. Thus after three months' deep thought he was able to readjust the seasons; to produce thunder in winter and ice in summer; to make creatures which walked upon the earth to fly, and birds to lose the use of their wings.

· Chung heu chin king. Keuen 2.

Q

To a man holding such beliefs the memory of the matter-of-fact Confucius, who had so steadfastly set his face against all superstitious follies, was naturally distasteful, and we find him constantly holding him up to ridicule and triumphantly contrasting the knowledge of uneducated lads with the so-called wisdom of the Sage. " One day," he tells us, " as Confucius was journeying in the East, he came upon two boys disputing. In reply to his questions as to the cause of their wrangling, one answered, ' I hold that when the sun rises in the east it is nearer to us than when it is overhead, and my reason for so thinking is that when it comes up it looks as large as the cover of a cart, and at noon it is no bigger than a wooden bowl.' ' I,' said the other, ' maintain that since the sun's rays, at rising, are cold and chill and at noon are hot, it follows that it is nearer to us at noon than in the morning.' Confucius was perplexed with the difficulty, and could give no decided answer. ' Where, then, is your great knowledge ? ' shouted the laughing boys after the retreating philosopher."

On the origin and nature of the universe, Leih-tsze differed lamentably from Laou-tsze, and enunciated a theory on the creation of the world which is quite unintelligible, and which is therefore here only literally translated. According to him, in the beginning was *Tai-yih*, or the Great Change ; *Tai-choo*, the Great Beginning ; *Tai-che*, the Great First ; and *Tai-soo*, the Great Pure. In the Great Change there existed no spirit. The Great Beginning was the origin of the spirit. The Great First was the beginning of form, and the Great Pure was the beginning of matter.

There was no separation between spirit, form, and matter, and all was chaos. And chaos was invisible, inaudible, and impalpable, and was therefore called *Yih*, "Change." And "Change" was without form and void; and Change underwent a transformation and became One. One was transformed and became Seven. Seven was transformed and became Nine, and Nine, the transformations having been exhausted, was retransformed and became One. One was the beginning of form. That which was pure and light ascended, and became heaven, and that which was impure and heavy became earth. It is impossible to treat seriously such strange wanderings of thought as these, but the fact of their having been gravely put forward by Leih-tsze helps to make intelligible the further fact that he believed in the magical wonders and tales of sorcery which he relates in his writings. When we meet with such statements, therefore, that kestrels become on occasions crow-pheasants, that swallows become frogs, and that field-mice become quails, we feel that there is no inconsistency in them.

Unfortunately, the influence of Leih-tsze's writings on the minds of his countrymen remains unaffected by the gross ignorance of the alphabet of physical and natural science which they display, and we are therefore unable to dismiss him as an author unworthy of notice. In many parts of his work he supports his views of man's place in the universe with vigour and grace. It is to this branch of his subject that his followers pin their faith, and it is this which has led them to exalt the indulgence of the licentious pleasures of the day to the highest place in their creed, and to throw aside every moral restraint as a folly. This phase of Leih-tsze's doctrines cannot be better illustrated than by a story he tells of Tsze-ch'an, a minister of the state of Ch'ing.[1] This man had, by a careful administration extending over three years, brought the state to a prosperous and peaceful condition. But his success in this respect was marred by the knowledge that his two brothers, Kung-sun Chaou and Kung-sun Muh, were devoting their lives to the grossest debauchery. As Confucius had laid it down as an axiom that before a man is fit to rule a state he must have succeeded in ruling his own family, Tsze-ch'an felt that it was contrary to Taou that his brothers should thus continue to outrage propriety ; and after consulting with a friend, he betook himself to his erring brethren, and addressed them, saying, " That which ennobles men above beasts is the possession of knowledge and forethought. Those virtues which follow from knowledge and forethought are propriety and righteousness. The perfection of these qualities gives reputation and position ; but he who indulges his passions, and pricks up his ears at licentious pleasures, will destroy his life. Now listen to me, and if by to-morrow morning you have repented of your ways, by the evening you shall be in office (lit. eat emoluments)."

To this the reprobates replied, " We have known all this a long time, and we have deliberately made our choice. Do you think we waited for you to tell us this ? Mortal life is difficult to get, but death comes

---

[1] Chung heu ching king.　Keuen 7, page 4.

easily enough. Who would spend a life which is difficult to get, in looking forward to a death which comes so easily? The desire to generate propriety and righteousness in order to vaunt ourselves before men, and to dissemble our appetites and natures to assume reputations, would be to us worse than death. Our object is to exhaust the dissipations of life, and to drink to the dregs the pleasures of the passing moment. Our only regret is that our capabilities forbid our drinking as deeply of licentious joys as we desire, and that our strength fails us before our passions are satisfied. We have no leisure to grieve over the disgrace which attaches to our name, nor to the dangers to our lives which we incur. And if you, who are so puffed up at being able to govern a nation, think to disturb our consciences by your sermon, and delight our imaginations by the prospect of glory and emoluments, you are playing a despicable and pitiable part. We will now point out to you the difference between our philosophy and yours. Your delight is in external government, and while you by no means are always successful, you inflict misery on your countrymen ; but we, who take pleasure in internal government, rarely give rise to disorder, and our natures revel in enjoyment. It is true your system of government may remain in operation for a time in a kingdom, but it will not be in harmony with the minds of the people. Our internal government, on the other hand, might be carried into effect throughout the empire, and then the Taou of rulers and ministers would have rest. We have long wished to impart this system to you, and do you venture to produce your scheme for our instruction?" Tsze-ch'an was dumbfounded, and had not a word to reply. But a day or two afterwards he told Tăng-seih what had passed. "You have been living with true men," said his adviser, "and did not know it. Who can call you wise? As to the order prevailing in the state of Ch'ing, that is a mere chance, and in no way attributable to your merit."

Such is the philosophy of Leih-tsze. How far it differs from the doctrines of Laou-tsze a comparison with this and the preceding chapters will show. Fortunately, though Leih-tsze stands high in the estimation of scholars, it by no means follows that they subscribe to his opinions. With the wonderful power the Chinese have of assimilating whatever in literature or science harmonizes with their own views, they have adopted just as many of the opinions of Leih-tsze as are not in opposition to the teachings of Confucius; the rest they treat as vain imaginings.

CHWANG-TSZE.

The remark of the celebrated commentator Choo He, that the disciples of Laou-tsze wandered further and further from his opinions as the period lengthened which separated them from him, does not hold good in the case of Lieh-tsze and Chwang-tsze. The preceding chapter will have shown how deeply Lieh-tsze erred in his views of Taouism; Chwang-tsze, on the other hand though far from being orthodox, kept more closely to the teachings of their common master. His compara-tive orthodoxy is admitted by Chinese scholars, and his great work, the *Nan hwa king*, is not unfrequently edited in conjunction with the *Taou tih king* of Laou-tsze. The vanity of human effort was his main theme, and the Confucianists were the principal objects of his denunciations. The fussy politician who boasts of having governed the empire is given to understand that the empire would have been very much better governed if it had been left alone, and the man who seeks to establish a reputation is told that reputation is but "the guest of reality." "The tailor bird builds its nest in the deep forest, but only on one bough; the field mouse drinks from the river, but only enough to satisfy his thirst."[1] Such are the examples which should be followed by men, and not the political purists and the ambitious ceremonialists. If the world were but left to itself, people would wear that which they spun and eat that which grew. The mountains would be without paths, and the waters without ships. All created things would rejoice in life. Wild animals would wander in troops, and trees and shrubs would flourish, among which birds and beasts might roam. Then would men enjoy a golden age. No knowledge would separate them from virtue, and no desires would taint their purity. But what is the state of things now? Sages turn round and round to become benevolent, and kick and struggle to become righteous, and people suspect them. They use frantic efforts to make music, and they bow and distort themselves in their endeavours to act with propriety, and the empire begins to break

[1] Nan hwa king. Keuen I.

up. Before cups of ceremony can be made, virgin timber must be spoilt. Before sceptres can be formed, white jade must be cut and shaped. If Taou and virtue were not corrupted, whence would there be such things as benevolence and righteousness? If the natural disposition had not been departed from, what use would there have been for ceremonies and music? If the five colours had not been thrown into confusion, whence would there have been lines and variations of colour? If the five sounds had not been thrown into discord, who could have echoed the six notes? The destruction of wood to make utensils is the crime of the workman, and the destruction of Taou and virtue to establish benevolence and righteousness, is the fault of the Sage." [1]

Thus Chwang-tsze was brought face to face in opposition to Confucius and to his own contemporary Mencius. Such men as these, he held, represented a disturbed order of things. When sages preached benevolence, it was a sure sign that evil was abroad, and when they talked of honesty, that robbery was rife. And in their own way they did as much harm in teaching men to depend on externals, and to force into unnatural channels the childlike nature of man as the worst of criminals. Mean men devote their lives to the acquisition of gain, scholars to obtaining reputation, and sages to governing the empire. But though the objects pursued by these men differ, and though they are called by different names, yet they all agree in doing violence to their natures. Pih E died for his

---

[1] Chwang-tsze.

good name at the foot of Mount Show-yang, and the robber Chih died through greed at the top of Tung-ling.   But though they sacrificed their lives for different objects, they agreed in having met with death and having outraged their natures.   Who will say whether Pih E was right, and whether the robber Chih was wrong?   All the world are greedy.   Some pursue benevolence and righteousness, and are called "superior men"; and others pursue goods and riches, and are called "mean men."   But they all seek after some object with greediness.[1]

The step from doubting the existence of any real difference in the motives of men to that of doubting the reality of one's own thoughts and feelings, and consequently of one's personal existence, is not a difficult one.   And Chwang-tsze was at one with the code of Menu, and pronounced the waking state one of deceptive appearances—a life among mere phantasmata.   On one occasion we are told he dreamt he was a butterfly, and that he was flitting about like a veritable insect, in complete oblivion of the existence of such an individual as Chwang-tsze.   But suddenly he awoke, and found himself in the person of Chwang-tsze.   The thought then occurred to his mind, "Was the vision that I was a butterfly a dream or a reality? or am I now a butterfly dreaming that I am Chwang-tsze?"[2]

But though there was this unreality in existence, life was yet a thing to be cared for.   Not as mean men, who are ever striving with fussy anxiety to add

Chwang-tsze.   Keuen 3.   [2] Chwang-tsze.   Keuen 1.

a few years to their lives, nor as the rich and great, who surround themselves with every luxury to nourish their bodies and every gratification to nourish their senses, forgetting that these are but as so many axes which before long will hew down the tree of life which they vainly hope to support ; but as the true Taouist, who, by seeking something beyond the body, nourishes the body.

"How best can I prolong my life?" asked the Emperor Hwan-te of the celebrated Kwang-ching-tsze. "By keeping yourself pure and still," answered the hermit ; "and above all things by avoiding lust. Let not the form of a woman meet your eyes, and let not the thought of her cross your mind. Of all the temptations men are heir to, she is the most dangerous. It is by following these rules that I have attained to my present advanced age."

This care for life, however, was quite compatible, according to Chwang-tsze, with an indifference for death ; and when his own end approached he met it with perfect calmness, telling his relations not to mourn over that which was inevitable. On the subject of his funeral he declared, " I will have heaven and earth for my sarcophagus, the sun and moon shall be the insignia when I lie in state, and all creation shall be the mourners at my funeral." When his relatives remonstrated, saying that the birds of the air would tear his corpse, he replied, "What matters it ? Above there are the birds of the air, and below there are the worms and ants ; if you rob one to feed the other, what injustice is there done ?"[1]

[1] Mayers's "Chinese Reader's Manual."

CHAPTER V.

LATER TAOUISM.

THE Chinese have no natural taste for philosophical speculations, and the Taouists, therefore, following the bent of their nature, threw aside the deeper musings of Laou-tsze with the same ease and indifference with which the followers of Confucius discarded the abstruser portions of the Confucian system. A few years sufficed to cast entirely into the background all metaphysical considerations enunciated by the old philosopher, and to construct out of the remnant of his teachings a system which might be applied to the practical concerns of life. How this new school came into existence, and who were its apostles, we have no means of knowing, but the fact that Che Hwang-te made an exception in favour of Taouist works when he ordered the destruction of the books, may possibly indicate that in the third century B.C. its adherents were a large and powerful body.

At a very early date the followers of Taou seem to have rejected Laou-tsze's doctrine of self-emptiness as insufficient to attract them, and to have sought to supplement it by making it a means to the attainment of everlasting life. The legend that Laou-tsze secured for himself immortality may have given rise to

this desire, or possibly, conversely, this desire may have
given rise to the legend of Laou-tsze's triumph over
death.   But, however that may be, we find that at the
time of Che Hwang-te, there was a very wide-spread
belief in the existence of charms which had the power
of conferring imperishable life.   Che Hwang-te himself was a firm believer in this and kindred superstitions.   He allowed himself to be persuaded into the
belief that in the eastern sea there were golden islands
of the blest, where dwelt genii, whose business and
delight it was to dispense to all visitors to their
shores a draught of immortality compounded of the
fragrant herbs which grew in profusion around them.
So sincere was his faith that he fitted out a naval
expedition to discover these much-to-be-desired
regions, and placed a professor of magical arts,
named Seu She, at the head of the undertaking.   On
the plea that it had been revealed to him that the
expedition was likely to meet with a more favourable
reception at the Golden Isles if a company of youths
and maidens accompanied it, Seu She persuaded the
emperor to send several thousands of girls and young
men with him.   On the return of the voyagers they
reported that they had sailed within sight of the
islands, but had been driven back by contrary winds.

Nothing daunted, the emperor despatched a second
expedition to bring back some of the waters of
life.   This also failed.   But private individuals
were, it is stated, more fortunate than the emperor,
and the people living on the sea-board of the
states of Ts'e and Yen—a part of the modern
provinces of Shantung and Chihli,—were visited

by numbers of travellers who had landed on the fairy islands, and who imparted to their country-men some of the secrets which had been communi-cated to them. Thus they learnt the arts of fusing metals, and of transforming themselves by the means of magical incantations. But no failure roused the emperor to a recognition of the imposture that was being played upon him. Countless sums were spent in vain, and profitless adventures at the command of Seu She, or other professors of magic. A pro-phetic announcement made to him that his dynasty would be overthrown by Hoo (the Huns) was suffi-cient to induce him to send an army of 300,000 men against those northern borderers. With the success-ful conclusion of the campaign the emperor believed he had falsified the prophecy, but the Taouists claim its fulfilment in the ruin which overtook the dynasty in the fall of his successor, Hoo Hai.

During the reign of Che Hwang-te the more eminent of the professors of the magical arts adopted for themselves the title of *Chin-jin*, or True men. These magicians professed to have mastered the powers of nature. They threw themselves into fire without being burnt, and into water without being drowned. They held the secret of the philosopher's stone, and raised tempests at their will. They were on terms of familiarity with the immortal inhabitants of the Isles of the Blest, who made known to them future events, and imparted to them the secret mysteries of Taou. But the time came when these men had to die, and as the acknowledgment of their deaths would have falsified their lives, it was

given out, as each disappeared from view, that he had
been carried off to some unknown paradise.

Not being willing to recognise for their religion a
foundation so modern as the time of Laou-tsze, the
Taouists claimed Hwang-te, the third of the mythical
five rulers, who is said to have ascended the throne in
the year 2697 B.C., as the real author of their faith,
and asserted that he never saw death, but was borne
away from the earth on the back of a dragon.
Unfortunately, however, the tomb of Hwang-te 'was
known to exist, and this discrepancy was urged on
the Taouists by the Emperor Woo, of the Han
Dynasty (140—86 B.C.), who seems to have imitated
Che Hwang-te in his patronage of the new sect. The
answer of the priests was that the court officials of
that day, being unwilling publicly to acknowledge his
translation, made a pompous funeral over the clothes
of their deified master, and that if the coffin were
opened its contents would substantiate their story.

Woo accepted this explanation, and allowed himself
gradually to fall under the entire dominion of the
priests. At first he was inclined to question their
statements, but by degrees so entirely did his judgment become perverted, that he reached a stage when
nothing became too hard for his faith. Like Che
Hwang-te he despatched several expeditions in quest
of the Fortunate Isles, but with no better success
than that which attended the efforts of his predecessor. He himself visited the Eastern Pung
Mountain, and was shown the footprints of a gigantic
genii who had appeared to the imperial professors of
magic in the preceding night in the form of an old

man leading a dog by a string. This was before his faith became unquestioning, and he ventured to throw doubts on the footprint. The professors, however, persisted in their statements, and, judging from the influence they subsequently gained over him, appear to have successfully deceived him.

At this time all traces of the Taouism of Laou-tsze had disappeared, and the attention of all his professed followers was directed to obtaining the elixir of immortality and the philosopher's stone. Death and poverty have always been regarded by man as the greatest evils under the sun, and in the dark and early ages of every nation's history sorcerers and alchymists have pretended to possess the arts of healing these sores of humanity. Like the Chinese Taouists, the European alchymists of the middle ages sought a high ancestry for their art. Noah was believed to have been acquainted with the *elixir vitæ*, and some were even bold enough to derive the first syllable of the word chemistry, and second of the word alchymy from the name of his son Shem, who was believed to have been an adept in the art. Moses also, said these writers, showed himself well versed in alchymy by being able to make the gold mix with or float on the water. In Rome and in Constantinople pretenders in the art of making gold and silver carried on a brisk trade during the first few centuries of the Christian era, and only a century ago Cagliostro and his wife reaped a golden harvest by the sale of the elixir of life at Brussels.

The mania for these magical arts among the Chinese during the Ts'in and Western Han dynasties

seems to have been as general and as acute as the
South-sea scheme madness among our forefathers.
From the emperors downwards, the people devoted
their lives to seeking immunity from death and
poverty. Business of every kind was neglected,
fields were left untilled, the markets were deserted,
and the only people who gained any share of the
promised benefits were the professors of Taouism,
who trafficked with the follies of their countrymen,
and who fattened on the wealth of the credulous.

Among the most credulous was the Emperor Woo,
who lavished money on all schemes suggested to him
by the professors of Taouism. It was only necessary
for them to tell him that Hwang-te had built such and
such temples in honour of the genii, and he instantly
gave orders for the erection of similar buildings. In
this way he was persuaded to build a palace, which
was to be a watch-tower for the genii, and entrance
to which was gained by a myriad of doors. In the gar-
dens surrounding it were ponds, in which swam fishes
and reptiles said to have been brought from the
Fortunate Isles, while large stone aviaries contained
birds of every shape and hue. He dedicated Mount
Tai to the worship of the genii, and raised a sacred
mound at the foot of the mountain. At the consecra-
tion of these holy places the emperor was present in
person, and during the night after the ceremony a
bright supernatural light rested on the mound which
had been made holy.

But it was obvious such an excess of zeal must be
short-lived. The numerous predictions and smooth
promises made by the Taouist priests must so often

have remained unfulfilled that even the most super-stitiously inclined must after a time have ceased to place any faith in them.   Death must have so often cast to the winds the anticipated length of days held out as a reward by the magician, and the professed power of manufacturing gold, must have so fre-quently proved itself to be an imposition, that no wonder people began to weary of a system which was so plainly a sham.

At this time Taouism was in no sense a religion, and exercised no control over the conduct of its votaries.   The court of the Emperor Woo was too often the scene of the grossest immorality, and Taouist writers recount without shame the legendary amour of the emperor with his fairy visitor Se Wang Moo. The only object of the priests was to trade on the uni-versal desire for wealth and long life, and he who professed the greatest powers received the greatest rewards.   "I know," said Le Shaou-keun to the emperor, "how to harden snow and to change it into white silver; I know how cinnabar transforms its nature and passes into yellow gold.   I can rein the flying dragon and visit the extremities of the earth ; I can bestride the hoary crane and soar above the nine degrees of heaven." And in return for these imaginary powers he became the chosen adviser of the emperor, and received the most exalted honours.

By the death of the Emperor Woo (B.C. 87) the magicians suffered an irretrievable loss.   Emperor after emperor arose after him who either withheld all patronage from them or gave them a very qualified support.   Neither did a change of dynasty restore

R

them to favour. They had had their day of unbounded imperial patronage, and to a faith in their
wild superstitious follies had succeeded a recurrence
to the ethics of Confucius and the mysticism of Laou-
tsze.   During the reign of the Emperor Hwan
(147–168 A.D.) great attention was paid to the system
of Laou-tsze, and it was during this period that the
custom of offering imperial sacrifices in the temple
dedicated to the old philosopher at K'oo Heen, the
supposed place of his birth, was begun.   Already,
however, there were traces of the influence of
Buddhism on the popular acceptance of the teachings
of Laou-tsze.   The duty of preserving life was held to
be among the leading doctrines of the philosopher.
Legends began, also, to appear of his career after
leaving the Han-koo Pass, which bear so striking a
resemblance to those met with in the life of Buddha,
that it is impossible to doubt the source from which
they were derived.   After passing out into the wild
country beyond the pass, Laou-tsze spent three nights
under a mulberry-tree, exposed to the temptations of
the evil one.   Lovely women tried to induce him to
accept their embraces, and, almost in the words of
Buddha, he rejected their advances.   "They are,"
said he, "but so many skin bags full of blood.   It is
by averting one's eyes from such, and by having
nothing to say to them, that Taou is perfected.   In this
age voluptuous girls and winsome women are looked
upon as the excellencies of the earth; while rich
living and choice wines have ruined the taste of the
empire."

For some centuries from this time Taouism remained neglected, and during the reign of Tai-keen (569–583 A.D.) an order was issued abolishing all religious orders, whether Buddhist priests and nuns, or Taouist doctors, and forbidding the promulgation of all doctrines but those contained in the Confucian classics. But after the death of this monarch brighter days dawned on these heretics, and under the Northern Wei Dynasty both Taouism and Buddhism received a share of imperial patronage. During the reign of the Emperor T'ai Wu-te (424–452) there was a return to the superstitious pursuit of the elixir of life and the philosopher's stone, and K'ow Keen-che, a Taouist doctor, became the confidential adviser of the emperor. At his instigation the emperor, in acknowledgment of the peace which his advice had gained for the empire, openly embraced Taouism, and at a solemn sacrifice accepted a magical charm as evidence of his adhesion to the doctrines of Laou-tsze.

By strict law the reception of such a charm was no light matter. The candidate, by the practice of benevolence, love, rest, and self-rectification, should have first gained for himself long life, and, having become a genii, have attained to incorporation in Taou. To each one who had thus perfected himself was given a charm, in the shape of a pure white book, in which were inscribed five thousand characters (the number of characters in the *Taou tih king*), consisting of the names of the officers of heaven, and certain incantations for deceiving demons, which were unintelligible to the laity. Before receiving the charm the recipient underwent a fast, and on the day of the ceremony he appeared bearing a present and a gold ring before

the priest, who received the present, and, having cut
the ring in two parts, returned one half to the recipient
of the charm, and kept the other half himself, as a
pledge of the vows taken by the saint. Together with
the charm was also presented, in some cases, a seal,
bearing the device of the sun, moon, and stars, which
enabled the holder to cure sickness, to tread on knives
without being cut, and to walk through fire without
being burnt.

These charms had been for more than a century in
vogue among the Taouists.   Like all the other superstitious excrescences on the doctrine of Taou, this one
was ascribed to Laou-tsze, and thus furnishes another
instance of the want of grasp of the teachings of the
" old philosopher " which Chinamen generally have
displayed.   To illustrate this, it is only necessary to
quote from the writings of Ko Hung, one of the most
celebrated doctors of Taouism during the fourth century, the purposes which the charms are said to serve.
" All mountains," he says, " are inhabited by evil
spirits, who are more or less powerful according to
the size of the mountain.   If the traveller has no protection, he will fall into some calamity.   He will be
attacked by sickness, or pierced by thorns, or witness
strange sights and sounds.   He will see trees moved,
but not by wind, and stones will fall without any
apparent cause from impending rocks, and will strike
him.   He will lose his way and fall down precipices,
or be assailed by wolves and tigers.   Mountains
should not be traversed in the winter—the third
month is the best time for such expeditions, and then
a lucky day should be chosen for setting out.   Fast-

ing and purification for several days beforehand is also necessary, and a suitable charm should be worn on the person."

"Sometimes a mirror is needed, for living things when they grow old can all, by means of their pure part, assume the human form. In such cases their true forms can be infallibly detected by means of a mirror, which should be nine inches in diameter, and suspended from the neck behind. These deceiving elves do not dare approach it; or if one should approach bent on mischief to the wayfarer, a glance in the mirror at the reflected image of the monster will reveal its true form. If it should be one of the genii, or some good spirit residing in the mountains, this, also, may be learnt by means of the mirror."[1]

In order to illustrate the importance of carrying these charms, the same writer relates the following adventure as a fact :—" Beneath the Lin-lu mountain was an arbour where a demon resided. Whenever a traveller lodged there he fell sick and died ; all night long forty or fifty persons of both sexes were to be seen there dressed in yellow, black, or white. Pih E one evening halted here for the night, and having lighted his candle sat chanting sacred books until midnight. A party of ten or more persons then arrived, and having seated themselves opposite the traveller began to gamble. Meanwhile Pih E secretly took his mirror and saw reflected in it an assembly of

[1] "Proceedings of the China Branch of the Royal Asiatic Society" (1855). Article on "Modern Development of Taouism," by Dr. Edkins.

dogs; so he took his candle and carried it so close to the clothes of one of the visitors as to burn them. When lo! the smell was as of scorched hair. He then grasped his knife and stabbed one of the demons. At the same moment a voice was heard crying out 'I am killed,' and immediately a dog lay lifeless on the ground. The others ran away."[1]

Such were the superstitious beliefs to which T'ai Wu te committed himself by the reception of the charms offered him by K'ow Keen-che, who taxed the credulity of his patron still further by professing to have gained the secret of the composition of the elixir of life. But the draught which he recommended to others failed to prolong his own days, and he died a victim of disease before he had attained any great age. But although the historians give us an account of his death-bed scene, and though there is preserved to us mention of the pompous funeral given to his remains at the command of the emperor, and of the Taouist ceremonies which were performed on the occasion, his followers stoutly affirm that he never saw death, but was carried up to heaven on the back of a dragon.

Already, as is indicated by the above superstition, there was a large admixture of Buddhist ideas with the popular notions. Coupled with the use of charms grew up also a system known as *Leen-yang*, or self-training, which consisted in the ascetic sitting cross-legged in an upright position; not that he might subdue

---

[1] "Proceedings of the China Branch of the Royal Asiatic Society" (1855). Article on "Modern Development of Taouism," by Dr. Edkins.

the flesh with the spirit and so become incorporated with Taou, nor that, like the Buddhists, he might win Nirvana, but that he might add years to his life, and rival the ages to which the Taouists of past times were said to have attained. This attitude was believed to promote longevity, since it tended to keep the breath in the lungs, and thus to ward off death, which is the final result of the unceasing expirations. The fact also of remaining still, and excluded from the world, helped to suppress that other enemy of life, the passions. And the ascetic, therefore, who sat in lonely silence in his solitary cave, overcame the process of decay which is natural to both the bodies and minds of men, and purchased for himself at the expense of all that makes life attractive, a few more years of ascetic penance. It is quite possible that such an existence may have tended to lengthen life, and that the belief that some of the early Taouists lived far beyond the ordinary span of man's existence may be quite true. We have it on record that Quakers are as a rule a long-lived people, and the fact is generally attributed to their avoiding all forms of excitement. In the same way the early Taouists who attained to the rest, purity, and the condition of inaction advocated by Laou-tsze, doubtless avoided much of the wear-and-tear which tends to shorten the days of those who fight their way in the arena of life.

The constitution, they held, is renewed every four-and-twenty hours, during which time a man makes 13,500 respirations, and as often therefore the constitution is drained. But that which is inhaled is the perfect breath of heaven and earth, and this, entering into the recesses of the body, not only prevents the constitution from wasting, but adds to the quantity and purity of the four elements (earth, water, fire, and air) of which the body is composed. When this condition of things prevails, the temper is cheerful, neither heat nor cold affects the health, and neither cares nor troubles harass the mind. The body is light, the bones strong, the breath vigorous, the spirit pure, and life becomes indefinitely prolonged.

On the other hand, if the source of life is not strong, the vital essence weak, and the breath feeble, the constitution wastes and is not replenished. The whole frame is out of keeping with nature, and instead of gaining the perfect breath of heaven and earth, it accumulates in itself an excess of the female principle of nature, and but a diminished quantity of the male principle. The consequence is that the breath becomes enfeebled, disease sets in, the breath is exhausted and the man dies.

Asceticism and public worship soon became engrafted on the doctrine of Laou-tsze, and the Emperor T'ai-ho (477—500) signalized his reign by building temples and monasteries for the Taouist doctors, in imitation of those of the followers of Buddha, which already were dotted over the empire. Indeed, the many outward resemblances which now existed between the rites and ceremonies of the Taouist and Buddhist sects led to constant wranglings and heart-burnings between the professors of the two creeds. The imperial patronage enjoyed by the Taouist magicians and alchymists was fiercely resented by the Buddhists, who pointed out that their opponents were nothing better than jugglers, while the Taouists retorted that the Buddhists were strangers in China, who, if they were not dealt with summarily, would inevitably cause disturbance by importing a foreign element into the empire.

Such was the condition of parties when Woo (566—578) ascended the throne, and so eager were both sides to gain the imperial support that, to satisfy them, the emperor summoned a conclave of 2,000 doctors and priests to argue on their relative systems and difficulties. After full deliberation the emperor gave his award and classed them both after Confucianism, and ranked Taouism before Buddhism. At this time the Buddhists had fallen away as much from the teachings of Buddha as the Taouists had from those of Laou-tsze, and the rites of both sects had become full of the grossest immoralities. This, coupled with the constant troubles to which their mutual jealousies gave rise, induced the emperor, not long after the conclusion of the conclave, to issue a decree abolishing both forms of worship. But this ban was again soon removed, and the Emperor Tsing (580-581) not only recognised both faiths, but ordained that in all temples in which stood images of Buddha and Teen-tsun " the Honoured one of Heaven," i.e. Laou-tsze, they should both be placed in equal positions of honour facing south.

With the accession of the Tang Dynasty, however, Taouism gained the advantage over its foreign rival. The delusions of the elixir of immortality and the philosopher's stone began again to exercise their

influence over the minds of men.   There are never
wanting knaves to take advantage of the weaknesses
of mankind, and so when this superstition revived,
magicians appeared also, who pretended to possess
the much-coveted secrets.   During the reign of Ching
Kwan (627—650) there arose, among a host of other
alchymists, a certain foreigner named Nabourh Sopo,
probably of Mongolian origin, who is said to have
concocted a draught of longevity.   Under the succeeding emperor (650—684) the Taouists still held
sway, and Laou-tsze received canonization by an
imperial decree, which proclaimed him to be Yuen
Yuen Hwang-te, *i.e.* the Emperor of the First Dark
Cause.   So great was the emperor's admiration for
him and for his teachings, that he ventured on the
daring innovation of including his writings in the
subjects of examination with the works of Confucius.
And not only so, but he insisted on his tributaries
taking up the study of Taouism.

Up to this time official posts had been conferred
only on Confucianists, but now not only Taouists, but
Buddhists also, were declared to be eligible for the
public service.   But in their turn they were con-
strained to conform to the Confucian rites, and a
special decree, issued by the Emperor K'ai-yuen
(713—742), bade them perform towards their parents
the filial duties inculcated by the Sage.   Following
the example set in the case of the principal disciples
of Confucius, K'ai-yuen canonized Chwang-tsze and
other followers of Laou-tsze, thus putting the sect in
all points on an equality with Confucianism.   He
also dabbled in alchymy, and roused the remon-

strances of his ministers by taking a dose of " Gold-stone Medicine." Thus nourished by imperial patronage, Taouist wonders became of frequent occurrence, and culminated in the appearance of Laou-tsze, who announced that if search were made in the Yin-he Pavilion in the Han-koo Pass, a charm of mystic efficacy would be discovered. By the emperor's orders a search was made, and it is need-less to add that a charm was found. Once again in the reign of this emperor, Laou-tsze appeared on earth, and in return for the favour thus shown him, the emperor canonized the saint under the title of the Great Sage Ancestor, and provided for the dis-tribution of the *Taou-tih king* throughout the empire. Under the remaining emperors of the T'ang Dynasty, Taouism received only occasional support, and at other times was the subject of persecution. During the reign of Paou-le (825—827) the Taouist doctors drew down the imperial wrath upon them by their intrigues and their pretensions, and were banished by a decree to the provinces of Kwang-tung and Kwang-se. But under Hwuy Ch'ang the tide turned again in their favour, and at their instigation Buddhism was officially stigmatized as a foreign religion.

During the whole of this period the discipline among the Taouist priests was extremely lax. The law, or rather the custom, which had grown up among them with the extension of Buddhism, and which forbade their marrying, was generally disregarded. In all social matters there existed no difference between them and the mass of the people. They married and brought up families, they farmed and frequented the markets, and placed themselves on a level with the ordinary traders in everything except the payment of taxes, from which they had been made exempt by the decrees of converted emperors. Under the first emperor of the Sung Dynasty (960—976), however, a return to a stricter system was enforced, and their priests were forbidden to marry. During the reign of Hwei-tsung (1101—1126) it was provided that the Buddhists should adopt Taouist names for the ranks of their hierarchy. Shakya was to be called *Teen-tsun*, "the Honoured One of Heaven"; a Buddha was to be *Ta-sze*, "Great Teacher"; a Lohan, *Tsun-chay*, "Honoured One"; and a Priest, *Tih-sze*. Certain Taouist priests were given official rank, and jurisdiction over their church.

The favour thus shown them by the emperors of the Sung Dynasty entailed on them persecution and loss when the Manchoos established the Kin, or Golden Dynasty over the north of the empire. To be the friend of the Sung was to be the enemy of the Kin Dynasty, and consequently the Taouists were looked upon with suspicion and aversion by the conquering Manchoos. Their freedom of movement was considerably curtailed, and all mandarins above the third rank were forbidden to hold any communication whatever with the priests of the sect.

But from the Mongols, who had been trained up in wild superstitions, the Taouists found ample support. No sooner did the armies of Jenghiz Khan appear on the northern frontier of the empire, than Taouist alchymists and magicians attached themselves to his banner. We read in history of prophecies uttered by these soothsayers being fulfilled, and of strange portents being explained. So great was the encouragement given to their arts, that various sects of Taouists sprang into existence, the followers of which all pretended to possess super-natural powers, and all received imperial patronage. It is related that when Kubilai's empress was ill on one occasion, the emperor summoned the Taouist priests to pray for her recovery, and that in answer to their supplications—to whom addressed we are not told—she recovered her health. In return for the service thus rendered, Kubilai conferred honours upon the priests, and gave largely in support of their temples and monasteries. In a note to his edition of Marco Polo, Colonel Yule says of the Taouists of this time, " On the feast of one of their divinities, whose title Williams translates as ' High Emperor of the Sombre Heavens,' they assemble before his temple, and having made a great fire, about fifteen or twenty feet in diameter, go over it barefoot, preceded by the priests, and bearing the gods in their arms. They firmly assert that if they possess a sincere mind they will not be injured by the fire ; but both priests and people get miserably burnt on these occasions. Escayrac de Lauture says that on those days they leap, dance, and whirl round the fire, striking at the devils with a straight Roman-like sword, and some-times wounding themselves, as the priests of Baal and Moloch used to do."

Thus, when in 1368 Hung-woo, the founder of the Chinese Ming Dynasty, came to the throne, he found the Taouists a powerful and favoured sect. And wisely judging it impolitic to declare himself hostile to so numerous a body, he determined to try to guide the current which he could not stem. He issued, therefore, decrees forbidding Taouist priests to live separately, or to wear red clothes, after the manner of the Mongolian Buddhists and Shamanists. He ordained also that all priests desiring official recognition should pass in the competitive examinations in the Confucian classics, that thus a bond of union might be maintained between them and the people of the empire. By Hung-woo's successors they were patronized or discountenanced according to the intelligence of the sovereign. Under Yung-lo, for example, their pretensions to supernatural powers were completely ignored, though the doctrines of Laou-tsze were duly respected. To an ambitious priest, who wished to persuade Yung-lo that the waters of longevity had a real existence, the emperor replied, " The only true means of acquiring longevity is to attain to purity of heart and freedom from desire"; thus plagiarizing the recommendation of Kwang-ching-tsze, uttered over four thousand years before, to those who wished to live long in the land. " Neither exercise your powers of sight nor of hearing, keep your bodies at rest and your minds at peace, and length of days will be your reward." .

Under Hung-che (1488—1506) the qualified support of the former emperors was exchanged for active hostility. The practice of alchymy was strictly forbidden as an absurd superstition, and the tenets of the sect were openly ridiculed by the emperor. Pointing to a burning temple on one occasion,

Hung-che said to the priest, "If those you worship were gods, would they allow their dwelling-place to be burnt down, or at least, would they not save themselves?" Though the same incredulity was not displayed by the succeeding emperors of the Ming Dynasty, Taouism did not receive the same support which had been accorded it by the Dynasty of Jenghiz Khan; and with the return of the Manchoos to power in 1636, even the limited patronage which had been extended to it was withdrawn. One of the first decrees of the Emperor Ts'ung-tih (1636—1644) was directed against Taouists, magicians, and other heretics, whose doctrines were held to be calculated to disturb the public mind, and who were therefore ordered to be suppressed. But such people die hard, and during the reign of K'anghe (1661 —1721) they were still practising their callings, and had become so formidable that that emperor determined to check their influence with the people. With this intention, he ordered that any magician or Taouist who should prescribe enchantments to recover people from illnesses should be sent to the Board of Punishments to be dealt with; and that any patient calling in the services of such quacks should be liable to punishment. And he further directed that all members of the " Do-nothing," the "White Lily," the "Incense-burners," the " Hung," the " Origin of Chaos," the " Origin of the Dragon," and the " Great Vehicle " sects, should be treated as criminals; and that all persons assembling for the purpose of reading the Sutras, or marching in procession bearing banners or striking bells, should be punished by flogging or wearing the cangue.

CHAPTER VI.

THE BOOK OF REWARDS AND PUNISHMENTS.

BUT though, as we have seen, modern Taouism has many points in common with Buddhism, it strikes off from it at the point where Buddhism runs counter to the tendency of the national mind. From the time of Confucius downwards the Chinese have been confirmed in their belief that the consequences of their acts on earth will not follow them beyond the grave, and that it is therefore in this life that they must expect to gain the advantages of virtuous conduct and to receive condemnation for unrighteous behaviour. In so far then as Buddhism treats of a heaven and a hell, Taouism has no fellowship with it, and on this point it is at one with Confucianism.

As in the case of Confucianism also, modern Taouism has discarded the abstruse philosophy and hard sayings of the *Taou tih king*, and has adduced from its pages a system of plain morality. And just in the same way as it may be said that the maxims of K'anghe embody popular Confucianism, so the *Kan ying peen*, or " Book of Rewards and Punishments," and the *Yin chih wăn*, or " Book of Secret Blessings," contain all that is considered by the people of the present day essential in Taouism.

The date of the first of these works is uncertain, but the claim which it puts forward to have had Laou-tsze as its author may safely be put on one side. It consists of two hundred and twelve maxims, which have been illustrated by short instances of personal narrative gathered from history up to the earlier part of the Ming Dynasty. We know also that it formed part of the grand collection of Taouist works which were published under the title of *Taou chang* in the latter part of the sixteenth century. The probability is, therefore, that it was published not earlier than the fifteenth or sixteenth century. But though lacking any but assumed antiquity, it has become, from the simplicity and practical wisdom of its teaching, to be the most popular of all the Taouist publications. So highly is it esteemed as a guide and instructor, that its distribution is considered to be a religious duty. Edition after edition appear from the local presses at the demand of charitable subscribers, who take means to disseminate copies among those who are too poor to buy them.

As this work is the one above all others which exercises influence over Taouists of the present day, we add a translation of the text :—

"Laou-tsze said, the bad and good fortune of man are not determined in advance ; man brings them on himself by his conduct. The recompense of good and evil follows as the shadow follows the figure."

' It is for this that there are in heaven and on earth spirits whose duty it is to search out the faults of men, and who, according to the lightness or gravity of their offences, reduce the length of their lives by

s

periods of a hundred days. When a period of a hundred days has been once diminished, poverty preys upon them little by little ; they are exposed to numerous miseries and difficulties ; men all hate them ; punishments and misfortune accompany them ; good fortune and happiness flee from them ; evil stars pour down calamities on them, and when all the periods of a hundred days are exhausted they die."

" There are also the Three Counsellors, and ' the Bushel of the North,' the Prince of Spirits, who are placed over men. They record their crimes and their faults, and deduct periods of twelve years and of a hundred days."

" There are also three spirits, called the *San chih*, who dwell in the bodies of men. When the *Kăng shin*[1] day comes, they mount to the palace of the heaven, and render their account of the crimes and the faults of men."

" On the last day of the month the Spirit of the hearth (who presides over the lives of all the members of the household) does the same."

" When a man commits a great fault, twelve years are deducted from his life ; when he commits a slight fault, a hundred days."

" There are several hundreds of great and little faults. Those who wish to gain immortality should avoid them in advance."

" Advance along the right way, and retreat from the evil way."

---

[1] The 53rd day of the cycle.

"Do not walk on a crooked path."

"Do not betray the secret of the household."

"Accumulate virtues, and hoard up merits."

"Be humane to animals."

"Practise righteousness and filial piety, be affectionate towards your younger brothers and respectful towards your elder brothers."

"Rectify yourself and convert men."

"Have pity for orphans, and show compassion to widows."

"Respect old men, and cherish infants."

"Do no injury, either to insects, plants, or trees."

"Pity the misfortunes of others."

"Rejoice in the well-being of others."

"Help them who are in want."

"Save men in danger."

"Rejoice at the success of others, and sympathize with their reverses, even as though you were in their place."

"Do not expose the faults of others."

"Never boast of your superiority."

"Prevent the evil, and exalt the good."

"Forego much, and take little."

"Receive princely favours with fear."

"Bestow favours without expecting recompense."

"Give willingly."

"A man who does these things is called virtuous. All men respect him. Providence protects him. Good fortune and office attend him. The demons flee from him. The god-like spirits guard him. He succeeds in all that he lays his hands to, and to him it is given the hope of immortality."

" He who wishes to become an immortal of heaven must do a thousand and three hundred good works. He who wishes to become an immortal of earth must do three hundred good works."

" He who entertains thoughts contrary to justice will act contrary to reason."

" (Do not) regard violence as a proof of ability."

" He who has an inhuman heart will treat others with cruelty."

" Don't inflict injury secretly upon the virtuous."

[" He who inflicts an injury in broad daylight," said Chwang-tsze, " will be punished by men ; but he who inflicts an injury in secret will be punished by demons."]

" Don't despise in secret your prince and your parents."

" Be not wanting in respect to your instructors."

" Don't rebel against those you serve."

" Don't take advantage of the ignorance of men to deceive them with lying words."

" Don't calumniate your fellow-students."

" Don't invent falsehoods, nor employ artifice and fraud."

" Never divulge the faults of your parents."

" Be not hard, violent, or inhuman."

" Never hastily satisfy your wicked caprices."

" Never confuse right and wrong."

" Learn to distinguish between friends who are to be sought and those who are to be avoided."

" Never ill-treat inferiors to gain merit."

" Don't flatter your superiors with the hope of gaining their favour."

" Be not forgetful of benefits."

" Do not cherish resentments."

" Do not think lightly of the lives of the people. "

" Do not introduce vexatious reforms into the administration of the empire."

" Don't reward the unrighteous."

" Don't punish the innocent."

" Don't commit murder for the sake of gain."

" Do not overthrow another, that you may take his place."

" Do not massacre the enemies who yield themselves, nor kill those who offer their submission."

" Do not exile the virtuous nor make destitute sages."

" Do not insult orphans nor oppress the widows."

" Do not violate the law and receive presents."

" Don't make crooked that which is straight, nor make straight that which is crooked."

" Don't rank faults as crimes."

" Don't indulge in anger in punishing a culprit."

" When you recognise a fault in yourself, correct it."

" When you know what is right, do it."

" Do not throw your own fault upon another."

" Do not throw obstacles in the way of the arts and trades."

" Do not throw contempt on and calumniate the holy men and sages."

" Don't insult and treat with cruelty those who study reason and virtue."

" Don't shoot at birds, nor hunt animals."

" Don't drive insects from their holes, nor frighten roosting birds."

" Don't stop up the holes of insects, nor destroy the nests of birds."

" Don't kill female animals great with young, nor break the eggs of birds."

" Don't wish misfortunes to others."

" Don't destroy the merit acquired by others."

" Don't expose other men to danger to secure your own safety."

" Don't seek your own advantage at the expense of others."

" Don't give bad merchandise in exchange for good."

" Don't give up the public good for private motives."

" Don't suck other men's brains."

" Don't conceal the virtues of others."

" Don't expose the defects of others."

" Don't reveal private affairs."

" Don't pilfer other people's goods and riches."

" Don't separate husband and wife, who are united as flesh to the bones."

" Don't help another to do evil."

" Don't give way to wilful passions, nor seek to impose by your power."

" Don't insult men to triumph over them."

" Don't destroy growing crops."

" Don't break asunder marriages."

" Don't make money improperly, nor pride yourself in your fortune."

" If you escape punishment by a piece of good fortune, yet blush for your crime."

" Don't usurp the advantages of others, nor throw the blame of your faults upon them."

" Don't give your own misfortunes in marriage to others, nor sell your crimes."

" Don't buy groundless praise."

" Don't hide within you a treacherous heart."

" Don't decry the excellences of others, nor conceal your own imperfections."

" Don't use your power to do violence to, or to oppress others."

" Don't give way to cruelty, to killing and wounding."

" Don't cut cloth without due cause."

" Don't kill and cook domestic animals except in accordance with the rites."

" Don't destroy or throw away the five kinds of grain."

" Don't harass and inflict suffering on men and animals."

" Don't ruin households, nor despoil men of their riches."

" Don't open the floodgates, nor start conflagrations to destroy the dwellings of others."

" Don't upset the plans and prospects of others to destroy their merit."

" Don't destroy men's tools [as for example the pencil of a scholar, the weapons of a soldier, the tools of a carpenter], so as to render them valueless."

" When you see others covered with glory and honour, don't desire to see them exiled from the country."

" When you see others possessed of riches, don't desire that they may lose them or dissipate them."

" Don't envy beauty."

" [A handsome figure excites the admiration of the world, but it does not deceive Heaven."]

" Don't desire the death of those to whom you owe money."

" Don't hate and curse those who are unwilling to satisfy your demands."

" Don't attribute the losses of others to their own faults."

" Don't laugh at the deformities of others."

" Don't put obstacles in the way of the promotion of men who are endowed with talents or worthy of praise."

" Don't bury the effigy of a man to inflict an incubus upon him."

[This refers to the practice of burying a wooden figure of a man to charm away his life, much in the same way that lately, in Shanghai and elsewhere, men were accused of making paper men which suffocated people in their sleep.]

" Don't use poison to kill your neighbour's trees."

" Don't harbour ill-feeling towards your instructors."

" Don't resist and offend your father and elder brothers."

" Don't delight in picking and stealing."

" Don't enrich yourself by robbery and violence."

" Don't seek to gain promotion by deceit and fraud."

" Don't complain that rewards and punishments are unjustly awarded."

" Don't give yourself up to ease and pleasure."

" Don't inquire minutely into the faults of inferiors and ill-treat them."

" Don't frighten and terrify people in distress."

" Don't murmur against Heaven at your lot, nor accuse men."

" Don't scold the wind, nor abuse the rain."

" Don't stir up strife and litigations between people."

" Don't enter the society of evil-doers."

" Don't listen to what your wife and concubines say."

" Don't disobey the instructions of your father and mother."

" Don't let new things make you forget the old."

" Never say anything you don't mean."

" Don't blindly covet riches, nor have recourse to fraud to deceive your superiors."

" Don't invent calumnies against innocent people."

" Don't defame others, and speak of yourself as upright and sincere."

" Don't abuse the spirits, and speak of yourself as a virtuous man."

" Don't renounce the duties prescribed by reason, nor learn to do that which is contrary to reason."

" Don't turn your back on your real parents, and seek parents at a distance."

" Don't take heaven and earth to witness the innocence of your criminal relations."

" Don't direct the penetrating glance of the gods on depraved actions."

" Don't give alms and afterwards regret having done so."

" Repay what you have borrowed."

" Don't seek to obtain anything beyond the lot appointed you by Heaven."

" Don't employ all your strength to accomplish your aims."

["The ancients said : 'If you have strength and power, don't employ them to the utmost.'"]

"Don't give yourself up beyond measure to pleasure."

"Don't assume a kind face, when there is cruelty in your heart."

"Don't give people foul food to eat."

"Don't mislead the multitude with false doctrines."

"Don't use a short foot, or an unfair measure, a light balance, or a small pint."

"Don't adulterate articles of merchandise."

"Don't seek after fraudulent profits."

"Don't force respectable people to follow vile callings."

"Don't deceive the innocent and set snares for them."

"Don't covet insatiably the property of another."

"Don't swear to your innocence before the gods."

"Don't love wine, nor abandon yourself to dissipation."

"Don't enter into angry disputations with your near of kin."

"If you would be a man, be sincere and upright."

"If you would be a woman, be gentle and obedient."

"Live in harmony with your wife."

"Wives, respect your husbands."

"Don't be always boasting."

"Don't indulge in jealousy and envy."

"Behave wisely towards your wife and sons."

"Wives, be not wanting in your duties towards your father- and mother-in-law."

"Don't treat with contempt the souls of your ancestors."

"Don't resist the orders of your superiors."

"Don't do anything which is not useful."

"Don't conceal a double mind."

"Don't utter imprecations against yourself and gainst others."

"Don't be unjust either in your love, or in your hate."

["If a man sees a Sage, he loves him; a vicious man, and he hates him. But if you hate any one unjustly, you close your eyes to his good qualities; and if you love with partiality, you blind yourself to his faults."]

"Don't leap over a well or a hearth."

["Wells and hearths are presided over by certain spirits, and if you leap over them, not only do you insult the gods, but you show that you have forgotten the two things which are the foundation of the life of men."]

"Don't pass either over food or over men."

["The *San kwan king* says, 'Those who have no respect for the grains, and who dirty them in passing over them, will be trampled upon' . . . Confucius said, 'He who carved the first men in wood, was deprived of posterity because he made them after the likeness of a man and used them at funerals.'"]

"Don't kill your children, either after their birth or before they have seen the light."

"Don't do anything clandestine or extraordinary."

["Confucius said, 'I don't imitate those who seek after hidden things, and who do strange things to divine the future.'"]

" Don't sing and dance on the last day of the month, or on the last day of the year."

["On the last day of the month the Spirit of the Hearth, who presides over the lives of men, ascends to heaven to make known their merits and faults. . . . On the last day of the year the Spirits of Heaven and Earth examine the virtues and the sins of men, to punish or recompense them."]

" Don't shout or get angry on the first day of the month, or in the morning."

" Don't weep or spit towards the north."

["The north is the place where resides the Prince of the Stars of the north ; the north pole is the hinge of Heaven. . . . If you dare to weep or spit towards the north, you outrage the gods and profane their presence, and you diminish the length of life which was accorded you by Heaven."]

" Don't sing or weep before the hearth."

" Don't burn perfumes with fire taken from the hearth."

" Don't prepare food with dirty wood."

" Don't rise up in the night naked and uncovered."

["The gods walk abroad during the night. Those who rise up in the night naked and uncovered commit a very grave crime."]

" Don't inflict punishments at the eight periods known as *Pa-tsieh*," *i.e.* 4th February, 21st March, 6th May, 21st June, 8th August, 23rd September, 8th November, and 22nd December.

["At each of these periods the Male and Female principles of nature succeed each other, and at the same time an analogous change takes place in the human body. If the punishment of flogging be inflicted at these times, the culprit not unfrequently dies under the chastisement."]

" Don't spit towards shooting stars."

[" These are phenomena which the Supreme Lord sends as a warning to men, and to turn them from their sins. Men ought therefore to be filled with fear, to practise virtue, and to offer sacrifices, to dissipate the calamities which threaten them."]

" Don't point at a rainbow."

[" When Confucius had finished the classic on Filial Piety, he observed a severe fast, and then turning towards the constellation of the North Bushel, he respectfully explained the motives with which he had composed his work. A red rainbow then fell from heaven, and changed into a piece of yellow jade, which Confucius received with a profound salutation."]

" Don't point rudely at the sun, moon, and stars."

" Don't stare at the sun or moon."

" Don't set fire to the brushwood in order to hunt in the spring."

[" Spring is the season when plants and trees begin to shoot, and then insects rear their young. At this time nature gives life and increase to all living things. If we cause these to perish, we rebel against Heaven, and destroy a multitude of its creatures."]

" Don't utter abuse towards the north."

" Don't needlessly kill tortoises and serpents."

[" The tortoise and the serpent answer to the constellation of the north known as Huen-woo. When, then, one kills these animals without legitimate excuse, one draws down on oneself terrible misfortunes."]

" The god which presides over the life of man inscribes all kinds of crimes, and according whether they are grave or light, he reduces the period of life by periods of twelve years or a hundred days. When the number of days is exhausted, the man dies ; and if at the time of his death there still remains any fault unexpiated, the punishment descends on his sons or grandsons."

" Whenever a man takes unjustly the riches of others, the spirits calculate the number of his wives and children, and cause them one by one to die until a kind of compensation is established. If the inmates of his house do not die, then disasters by fire and flood, by thieves, by cheats, by loss of effects, by sickness, by slander or denunciation, will wipe off an equivalent of that which he has taken unjustly."

" Those who kill innocent people are like enemies who exchange weapons and kill one another."

" He who takes unjustly the riches of another, is like a man who tries to appease his hunger with tainted meat, or his thirst with poisoned wine. Although he thrives on it for the moment, death is sure to overtake him."

" If you form in your heart a good intention, although you may not have done any good, the good spirits follow you. If you form in your heart a bad intention, although you may not have done any harm, the evil spirits follow you."

" If a man who has done wrong repents and corrects himself, if he abstains from evil deeds, and accomplishes all sorts of good works, he will at length obtain joy and felicity. This is called changing evil fortune for good."

"A good man is virtuous in his words, looks, and actions. If each day he practises these three virtues, at the end of three years Heaven will pour down blessings upon him. The wicked man is vicious in his words, looks, and actions. If each day he practises these three vices, at the end of three years Heaven will send misfortunes upon him."

"Why then do we not force ourselves to do good?"[1]

[1] "Le Livre des Récompenses et des Peines." Traduit par Stanislas Julien.

CHAPTER

THE BOOK OF SECRET BLESSINGS.

IN the *Yin-chih-wăn* also, there is no reference whatever to the doctrines of Taouism, but only a number of moral injunctions of great ethical purity. The work is popularly believed to have been written by the deity Wăn-chang Te-keun, but the name of the real author is unknown. The benevolent spirit which runs through its pages has caused it to be welcomed by Buddhists, Confucianists, and Taouists alike; and next to the *Kan-ying-peen* it is the most popular religious work in China.

Its teachings rest on a sound foundation where they inculcate the necessity of purifying the heart as a preparation for all right-doing. Be upright, it says, and straightforward, and renew your heart. Be compassionate and loving. Be faithful to your master, and filially pious to your parents. Honour your elder brethren, and be true to your friends. Help the unfortunate; save those who are in danger; and set free the bird taken in a snare. Have pity towards the orphan and the widow; honour the aged, and be kind to the poor. Feed the hungry; clothe the naked; and bury the dead. Use just weights and measures, and do not overtax the people. Succour the sick, and give drink to the thirsty.

Redeem the lives of animals, and abstain from shedding blood. Be careful not to tread upon insects on the road, and set not fire to the forests, lest you should destroy life. Burn a candle in your window to give light to the traveller, and keep a boat to help voyagers across rivers. Do not spread your net on the mountains to catch birds, nor poison the fish and reptiles in the waters.

Never destroy paper which is written upon; and enter into no league against your neighbour. Avoid contentions, and beware not to stir up ill blood. Use not your power to discredit the good, nor your riches to persecute the poor. Love the good, and flee from the face of a wicked man, lest you fall into evil. Hide your neighbours' faults, and speak only of their good deeds, and let your mouth utter the true sentiments of your heart. Remove stones and débris from the roadway, repair the footpaths, and build bridges.

Publish abroad lessons for the improvement of mankind, and devote your wealth to the good of your fellow-men. In all your actions follow the principles of Heaven, and in all your words follow the purified heart of man. Have all the Sages of antiquity before your eyes, and examine carefully your conscience. What good thing will be withheld from him who practises " secret benefits" ?

Such are some of the leading maxims of this pamphlet, which consists of only five hundred and forty-one words, but which has exercised, and is still exercising, an influence out of all proportion to its

T

bulk. It has gone through many thousand editions, and has become a household word throughout the empire. Benevolent people distribute copies gratis in the streets, and the zeal of engravers and commentators has increased its proportions to the size of a goodly volume.

These two works may fairly be taken to represent the moral side of modern Taouism. Few professing Taouists trouble themselves at the present day about the musings of Laou-tsze, or the dreamy imaginings of his early followers. They pursue only their own good, mainly temporal, but also moral. To secure the former they have recourse to the magical works of the sect, and to the expounders of these, the Taouist priests. They buy charms and practise exorcisms at the bidding and for the profit of these needy charlatans, and they study with never-failing interest the advice and receipts contained in the numberless books and pamphlets published for their benefit.

Into some of these, Buddhist ideas are largely imported, and the doctrine of the existence of hell, which finds no kind of canonical sanction, is commonly preached. Liturgies, also framed on Buddhist models, abound, and in some cases not only the form, but even the phraseology of Hindoo works, is incorporated into these prayer-books.

CHAPTER VIII.

TAOUIST DEITIES.

WE have already referred to the intimate connection which exists betweet Taouism and Buddhism, and in nothing is this more apparent than in the Taouist Pantheon. Laou-tsze, the founder of the religion, knew nothing of gods and goddesses, and it was not until the introduction of Buddhism that his followers set up for themselves shrines and images. Naturally, the first person to be deified was Laou-tsze, and, following the example of the Buddhists, who worship Sakyamuni in three persons, as the Tathagatha of the three ages—the past, the present, and the future,— they enthroned Laou-tsze as the highest object of worship, under the title of San tsing, or "the three pure ones." Each person of this trinity is represented by an image, and, just as when one enters a Buddhist temple thè three representations of the Tathagatha of the three ages meet one's eye, so in Taouist "palaces" Laou-tsze in his triple form is the principal object.

But though Laou-tsze is the first object of reverential worship, he is too purely the representative of abstract contemplation to allow of it being considered possible that he should take cognizance of things which are of the earth, earthy. It was necessary,

T 2

therefore, to introduce a god who, as the ruler of the world, should undertake direct superintendence of the affairs of men, and to whom they might convey their hopes and their griefs. Such a being they invented under the title of Yuh-hwang Shang-te, or "the Precious Imperial God," who governs the physical universe. As time went on, and magicians and alchymists began to flourish, the idea that everything in nature consists of two parts, matter and its essence, gave rise to the belief that the stars were the sublimated essences of things, and as such were to be regarded as gods, and as worthy of association with Yuh-hwang Shang-te. The earth, it was said, is composed of five constituent parts, viz., metal, wood, water, fire, and earth, which are represented in the heavens respectively by the planets Venus, Jupiter, Mercury, Mars, and Saturn. Many other stars have in the same way been deified, and are believed to exercise a direct and powerful influence over the affairs of men. Thus the Taouist sees in the heavens an etherealized counterpart of the world around him, and as he believes that the relation between these two parts is as close as that between body and soul, he has learnt not only to worship the essences, but to bow down before the physical objects, such as the mountains, the valleys, the streams and the rivers, which they represent.

The Great Bear comes in for a large share of the star-worship, one part being supposed to be the palace of a female divinity known as Tow-moo, and another part being dedicated to the god Kwei-sing. The powers of nature are also plenteously represented in the mythology. The God of Thunder is a common object of worship, "and is represented as passing through many metamorphoses and filling all regions with his assumed forms. While he discourses on doctrine his foot rests on nine beautiful birds. Thirty-six generals wait on him for orders. A certain celebrated book of instruction is said to have emanated from him. His commands are swift as winds and fire. He overcomes demons by the power of his wisdom, and he is the father and teacher of all living beings."[1] Among other like deities are, "the Mother of Lightning," "the Spirit of the Sea," "the King of the Sea," and "the Lord of the Tide." The temples of the Dragon King are also favourite resorts of worshippers, who in all convulsions of nature recognise the agency of this potent and amphibious monster. Serpents are looked upon as manifestations of this deity, and in times of flood often receive worship at the hands of the educated and the uneducated alike. During the flood which overspread the country round Tientsin in the year 1874, a serpent sought shelter in a temple near the city, and ensconced himself beneath one of the altars. Far from desiring to get rid of the intruder, the priests welcomed it as a sacred guest of good omen, and Li Hung-chang, the viceroy of the province, came in person to pay reverence to it as the personification of the Dragon King.

But apart from these more general deities are gods who preside over the different pursuits and callings of men. As the number of deities is practically unlimited, and as it is obviously to the interest of the priests to

[1] Edkins's "Religion in Chian.'

encourage worship of whatever kind at their temples, there has never been any difficulty in adding a god or two to the Pantheon. Thus students have chosen to appropriate to themselves a god, who is supposed to watch over the literary efforts of his votaries. *Wăn-ch'ang te keun*, or the god of literature, is, according to legend, the disembodied spirit of Chang Chung, an official of the Chow Dynasty. Under subsequent dynasties he appeared on earth in the persons of men renowned for their scholarship and virtue, and finally, under the Yuen Dynasty, he was deified under the title of " Supporter of the Yuen Dynasty, diffuser of renovating influences, Sze-luh of Wăn ch'ang, God and Lord."

Since his apotheosis he has received official worship throughout the empire. Twice on each year, namely on the 3rd day of the second month, and again during the eighth month, sacrifices and invocations are offered to him on every altar by representatives of the emperor, when the following prayer is read by the official appointed for the purpose :—

On this —— day of the —— moon, in the year ——, the emperor despatches his officer named —— to offer sacrifices unto the god Wăn ch'ang, and to say :—O Divine Being ! Thou who didst manifest thy presence at Tung in the western region ; whose [star, the] pivot [of the firmament] doth make the circuit of the northern pole ; who shineth brightly in the sixfold constellations ; who orderest the splendour of auspicious fates.

"From generation to generation thou hast sent thy miraculous influence down upon earth. Thou hast been the Lord and Governor of learning among men. In upholding that which is right, long hast thou brightly shone and stirred up hearts to thankfulness. It is meet that a tribute of reverence and worship be paid with sweet-scented offerings. Now, therefore, at this period of mid-spring (or mid-autumn) it behoves us to fulfil the season's adoration. May the fumes of this sacrifice, and the odour thereof, be acceptable to thee! Look down, we beseech thee, on our devotion and our humility."[1]

The worship thus offered by the emperor is reflected among the people at large. In every city temples built by private munificence or by subscription are dedicated to the honour of Wăn Ch'ang, in which Taouist priests and fortune-tellers ply their trades with never-failing success. In some cases the temples are built adjoining the colleges set apart for literary study, in order that the students may have ready access to the shrine of the deity on whose smile or frown depends their success or non-success at the competitive examinations. In the principal hall of the temple stand an altar and shrine, the interior of which "is occupied by a venerable figure, seated in calm and dignified repose, a benign expression manifested in the gilded features, and a flowing beard descending to the lap, upon which the hands lie folded. In front stand the narrow perpendicular tablets, set in deep frameworks of elaborate carving, which indicate the titles of the object of worship."

At Canton there are no fewer than ten such temples,

[1] "Journal of the North China Branch of the Royal Asiatic Society." New Series, No. 6.

all of which are constantly attended by ambitious students or their relatives. At Choo-tung-yun, where Wăn-ch'ang is said to have been born, stands the principal temple devoted to his honour. On one of the central beams of this building stands a brazen eagle, from the bill of which a string hangs down in front of the altar. Tied to the string is a pencil, with which the god is said to write words of mystic meaning on a table covered with sand. These heavenly messages are generally prophetic announcements of impending misfortunes; and it is said that in 1853 an intimation of this kind was sent by the priests of the temple to the celebrated viceroy Yeh, warning him of the political troubles which were beginning to disturb the provinces.[1]

Soldiers, again, worship Kwan-te, the God of War, who when on earth bore the name of Kwan yu. In early life he carried on the trade of selling bean-curd, but having a soul above so mean a calling, and the times in which he lived (under the Han Dynasty, during the second century) being favourable to ambitious enterprise, he embarked on the career of a soldier of fortune, and won for himself both honour and renown. He lived to receive the title of Baron, but being entrapped by a crafty enemy, he was taken and beheaded. For many centuries his name remained embalmed only in history, but during the twelfth century he was canonized under the title of Chung-hwuy Kung, "the Patriotic and Clever Duke," and a little later he was promoted to the rank of Prince. But it was reserved for the Emperor Taou-

[1] Gray's "China."

kwang to proclaim his apotheosis. After the sup-
pression of the Mahommedan rebellion under Changkihur in 1828, the emperor published the following
decree :—

"Ever since the tripod of our dynasty was firmly
established, his majesty Kwan-te has often gloriously
displayed spiritual and divine aid.

"Chang Ling, the commander-in-chief, reported
last year that when the rebels, headed by Changkihur,
advanced towards Aksu, and were attacked by our
troops, a gale of wind suddenly arose, filling the air
with flying sand and dust. Then the rebels saw in
the distance a red flame illumining the heavens, and
they were either slain or taken prisoners.

"On another occasion, whilst Chang Ling was
leading on the imperial forces at Hwan river, the
rebels annoyed the camp during the whole night, till
a violent tempest arose, which enabled our troops to
dash in among the rebels without being perceived,
when an innumerable multitude of them were taken,
and had their ears cut off.

"The next morning the rebels all confessed that
they saw in the midst of a red flame large horses and
tall men, with whom they were utterly unable to contend ; and hence they were obliged to flee.

"All these manifestations have proceeded from our
looking up and relying on the spiritual majesty and
glorious terror of Kwan-te, who silently plucked away
the rebels' spirits, and enabled us to seize alive the
monster of wickedness (Changkihur), and so to
eternally tranquillize the frontier.

"It is therefore right to increase our sincere devotion to Kwan-foo-tsze, in the hope of insuring his protection and the tranquillity of the people, to tens and hundreds of thousands of years.

"I therefore hereby order the Board of Ceremonies to prepare a few words to add to the title of Kwan-foo-tsze, as an expression of gratitude for the protection of the god. Respect this."

Once again, in 1855, when the followers of the Tai-ping chief were carrying fire and sword through the central provinces of the empire, Kwan-te fought on the side of the imperial troops, and caused them to inflict a severe defeat upon the rebel host. For this act of mercy the reigning Emperor, Heen-fung, published a decree in which he commanded that the same divine honours which are paid to Confucius should be paid to Kwan-te. It is difficult to determine how far this faith in the deity on the part of the authorities is real, and how far it is feigned. The majority of educated men regard such beliefs as popular superstitions, but notwithstanding this, the Government is willing to make use of them to support its authority by persuading the people that even the gods fight against the opponents of the Great Pure Dynasty.

But probably no god is worshipped with greater fervour than is Tsai-shin, the God of Riches. Though the pursuit of riches and honour is discountenanced by all the leading Taouist writers, the natural desire for wealth has overcome all religious warnings and denunciations, and is as strong among the Taouists of China as among the most money-loving nation in the world. No god can boast more temples raised to his honour than Tsai-shin. Every trader who at the end of the year finds the balance of his accounts in his favour, acknowledges the mercy shown him by making a votive offering to the dispenser of wealth ; and he who fears a loss attempts to propitiate the god by sacrifices and gifts.

As bestowers of earthly benefits, the three subordinate star gods, in whose hands rest the blessings of happiness, rank, and old age, naturally find great favour among the essentially worldly Chinamen. Buddhists may preach of the happiness of Nirvana, and Taouists may expatiate on the advantages of incorporation in Taou, but the practically-minded Chinaman leaves the pursuit of these abstractions to those who preach, and devotes his attention to the acquisition of the blessings more immediately within his reach. If the Taouist temples had no niches for the gods of wealth, rank, happiness, and old age, the priests would make but a poor living, and three-fourths of the temples throughout the land would be deserted.

It will be observed that there is nothing distinctively Taouist in the worship of these gods except the gross superstition which accompanies it, and it is evidence of the present very degraded condition of Taouism that, whenever a popular deity has to be enthroned, Taouist priests are the servitors chosen to wait upon his shrine. Combined with the office of guardian, these backsliding charlatans ply the trades of fortune-tellers, prophets, and doctors. If a merchant wishes to know whether a venture will turn out profitably or the reverse, or if a mother wants to be assured whether her infant's future is to lie among the blessings of office, wealth, and long life, or to be accompanied by poverty and misfortune, they betake themselves to a Taouist priest, who, well versed in the tricks which ape superhuman knowledge, returns oracular responses, which satisfy, for the time being at least, the superstitious wants of the applicants. Nor is their medical advice based on any surer basis. Dr. Gray, in his recent work on China, gives the following description of an incident he witnessed at a temple in Canton:—" Whilst I was visiting one of these temples, a father brought his son to the priests . . . saying that the child was possessed of a devil. Having consulted the idol, the priests informed him that there were 'no fewer than five devils in the body of his son, but that they were prepared to expel them all on the payment of a certain sum. The father agreed. The child was then placed in front of the altar, and on the ground near his feet were placed five eggs, into which the priests adjured the devils to go. As soon as they were supposed to have entered the eggs, the chief of the priests covered them over with an earthenware vase, and at the same time sounded a loud blast upon a horn. When the vase was removed, the eggs, by a trick of legerdemain, were found no longer on the ground, but in the vase. The priest then proceeded to uncover his arm, and made an incision with a lancet on the fleshy part. The blood which flowed from the wound was allowed to mingle with a small quantity of water in a cup. The seal of the temple, the impression of which was the name of the idol, was then dipped into the blood and stamped upon the wrists, neck, back, and forehead of the poor heathen child, who was suffering from an attack of fever and ague."

Among the multitude of other gods which claim the allegiance of modern Taouists are the three celestial intendants, who are more purely sectarian. Tsze-wei te-keun, the intendant of heaven, is the distributor of happiness; the second, Tsing-ling te-keun, the intendant of earth, is the pardoner of offences; and the third, Yang-kow te-keun, the intendant of water, is he who delivers from danger. Besides these are the *San tai'*, or three counsellors who watch over the actions of each person individually. They preside over the life and over the death of each, over length of days and shortened careers. There are the *San chi*, whose duty it is to register the deeds done by every one, whether they be good or evil. There is the god of the hearth, who has charge of the household generally, and of each member of it separately; besides very many others.

Inferior only to these deities is the Hierarch of the Faith, who lives in considerable state in the *Lung hu shan*, or Dragon and Tiger Mountains, in the province of Kiang-se. It is believed that this prelate is the earthly representative of Yŭh-hwang Shang-te, who is but the ascended form of one of his ancestors. - Since the apotheosis of this saint, there has not been wanting a member of his clan to sit upon the priestly throne. As in the case of the Lama of Tibet, the appointment is officially made among the members of the clan by lot. On the day appointed for the election, all the male members of the clan assemble at the priestly resi-

dence, when a number of pieces of lead, each bearing
the name of one of those present, are thrown into an
earthenware vase filled with water.   Around this
stand priests, who invoke the " Three Pure Ones " to
cause the piece of lead bearing the name of the person on whom the choice of the gods has fallen to rise
to the surface of the water.[1]   The result of the election is reported to the emperor, in whose hands rests
the confirmation of the appointment.   Nominally the
authority of this hierarch is supreme among the priests
of the sect throughout the empire, but practically he
seldom interferes with his subordinates.   The present
hierarch is said to be a very ordinary man, with but
slight culture, and with as little sense of the dignity of
his office.

The mental and moral state of this man is a fitting
representation o the condition of modern Taouism in
China.   Every trace of philosophy and truth has disappeared from it, and in place of the keen searchings
after the infinite, to which Laou-tsze devoted himself,
the highest ambition of his priestly followers is to learn
how best to impose on their countrymen by the vainest
of superstitions, and to practise on their credulity by
tricks of legerdemain.   By the educated classes they
are looked down upon with supreme contempt, and
only such of their beliefs as have received the approval of the Government at different times for various
causes, are in any way recognised by any but the most
ignorant of the people.   By law, candidates for the
priesthood should go through a course of study ex-

[1] Dr. Gray's " China."

tending over five years, at the end of which time they take the vows, and receive a licence from the local mandarins. But practically their novitiate is spent in serving the priests, who impart to them only such knowledge of chicanery and fraud as they themselves possess, and a smattering of ethical science, to enable them to prompt the oracular responses of the gods to the inquiries of the sick and dying. The social morality of the priests is of the most degraded kind, and the nunneries, which, in imitation of the Buddhists, they have established throughout the empire, are by common report described as the haunts of every vice. Without a belief in any god apart from deified men, without the purer motives which influence the Buddhists in their endeavours to reach a higher life, having drifted, century after century, farther and farther away from all that is noble, unselfish, and true, the modern Taouists have sunk lower in the estimation of their fellow-men than any but the most degraded of idolaters.

THE END.

Richard Clay & Sons, Limited, London & Bungay.

Non-Christian Religious Systems.

Fcap. 8vo., cloth boards, 2s. 6d. each.

BUDDHISM—Being a Sketch of the Life and Teachings of Gautama, the Buddha. By T. W. RHYS DAVIDS, M.A., PH.D. A New and Revised Edition. With Map.

BUDDHISM IN CHINA. By the Rev. S. BEAL. With Map.

CHRISTIANITY AND BUDDHISM—A Comparison and a Contrast. By the Rev. T. STERLING BERRY, D.D.

CONFUCIANISM AND TAOUISM. By Professor ROBERT K. DOUGLAS, of the British Museum. A New and Revised Edition. With Map.

HINDUISM. By the late Sir MONIER WILLIAMS, M A., D.C.L. A New and Revised Edition. With Map.

ISLAM AND ITS FOUNDER. By J. W. H. STOBART. With Map.

ISLAM AS A MISSIONARY RELIGION. By C. R. HAINES. [2s.]

STUDIES OF NON-CHRISTIAN RELIGIONS. By ELIOT HOWARD.

THE CORÂN—Its Composition and Teaching, and the Testimony it bears to the Holy Scriptures. By Sir WILLIAM MUIR, K.C.S.I., LL.D., D.C.L.

THE RELIGION OF THE CRESCENT; or, **ISLAM,** its Strength, its Weakness, its Origin, its Influence. By W. ST. CLAIR TISDALL. [4s.]

SOCIETY FOR PROMOTING CHRISTIAN KNOWLEDGE,
LONDON: NORTHUMBERLAND AVENUE, W.C.

Printed in the United States
61162LVS00004BA/5

9 781417 977680